HOW TO
start & run
an
Investment Club

for fun & learning

**CANADIAN
SECURITIES
INSTITUTE**

**Investor
Learning
Centre**
OF CANADA

Toronto • Montreal • Calgary • Vancouver

Names of individual securities mentioned in this text are for purposes of example only and are not to be construed as recommendations for purchase or sale.

Prices of individual securities given in this text are for the purposes of comparison and illustration only and were approximate figures for the period when the text was being prepared. Current quotations may be obtained from the financial pages of daily newspapers or the financial press or from your Investment Advisor.

While information contained in this text has been obtained from sources the publisher believes to be reliable, it cannot be guaranteed nor does it purport to treat each subject exhaustively.

This publication is designed to provide accurate and authoritative information in regard to the subjects covered. It is distributed with the understanding that the Canadian Securities Institute and the Investor Learning Centre of Canada are not engaged in rendering legal, accounting or other professional service. If legal advice or other expert assistance is required, the services of competent professional persons should be sought.

**CANADIAN
SECURITIES
INSTITUTE**

121 King Street West
Suite 1550
Toronto, Ontario
M5H 3T9

Tel: (416) 364-9130
Fax: (416) 359-0486
internet: www.csi.ca

Canadian Cataloguing in Publication Data

Main entry under title:

How to start and run an investment club

Includes index.
ISBN 1-894289-04-8

1. Investments clubs – Canada – Management. I. Canadian Securities Insitiute.

HG4530.H682 1998   332.6   C98-932403-6

First Printing 1998 by the Canadian Securities Institute.

Copyright 1998, by the Canadian Securities Institute.

Printed and bound in Canada by Key Interactive Inc. A Dollco Communications Company.

Acknowledgements

This book was developed by the public education creative unit of the Canadian Securities Institute (CSI) in response to the many individuals who over the years have sought information about investment clubs from the CSI and its sister organiza-tion the Investor Learning Centre of Canada (ILC).

A number of talented and dedicated people have played key roles in the writing, design and production of this book. Consultant Michael Bowness was art director and provided all the illustrations. Marthe Yolleck carried out the desktop design. Consultant Chuck Midgette wrote several sections and initiated the style and tone for the finished work.

Several others contributed ideas, reviewed sections and proof-read the manuscript, including: Mike Pickett, CSI vice-president of research; Ann Clarkson, CSI and ILC vice-president of marketing communications and public education; Michael Terry, CSI production manager; Catherine Shearer-Kudel, CSI public education specialist; Dawn Marchand, CSI marketing communications manager; and, Jacqueline Watts, marketing communications coordinator for the ILC.

Most of all, acknowledgement belongs to Dr. Roberta Wilton, president of the CSI and ILC, whose idea it was to produce this book and who throughout has been a steadfast supporter of this project, and others aimed at helping ordinary Canadians become better investors.

Dominic Jones
Editor

Preface

How to Start and Run and Investment Club for Fun and Learning is divided into eight sections, each built loosely around the eight easy steps you need to get your club up and running smoothly.

Step One: Establish your club's goals and investment philosophy. Being clear about your goals is crucial to your club's long-term success. You'll learn how to assemble of group of like-minded people and decide on your club's main purpose, which usually is to learn about investing by actually doing it. You'll establish an investment strategy suitable for all members' needs, such as a buy-and-hold approach.

Step Two: Formalize your club structure. Sign the interim constitution included at the back of this book and you're on your way. You'll learn about a little-known provision of Revenue Canada called the "modified partnership" that greatly reduces the time and hassle you'll have reporting club income on members' tax returns. At the back of the book, you'll find a letter informing Revenue Canada of your club's decision to be taxed as a modified partnership. All that's left to do is choose a distinct name for your club and — presto! — you've got your own investment club.

Step Three: Elect office holders. Somebody's got to bear responsibility for carrying and assigning the club's diverse duties. You'll need a president, vice-president, secretary and — above all — a treasurer to take care of the club's affairs. The book explains the key attributes needed for each of these positions and describes the nominating and voting procedures for electing club officials.

Step Four: Open a bank and brokerage account. Once you have officers, it's time to sort out who is going to have authority to write cheques and issue trading instructions to your brokerage firm. The book also explains how to go about selecting a suitable broker, and gives handy tips on the benefits of getting on-line access to your club's account.

Step Five: Draft a monthly meeting agenda. You'll need an agenda for each of your meetings that allows time for education and for members to make presentations on potential new investments. Guidelines are provided for how to make an effective presentation on a new investment, including a standard tracking form for monthly reviews of each investment your club owns.

Step Six: Set up a flexible accounting system. Once you start investing your club's money, you'll need a system to keep tabs on how that money is doing. The unit value accounting system is easy to set up and maintain, and best of all it's flexible enough to accommodate just about any eventuality that might happen upon your club, including adding new members and saying goodbye to old ones. You'll also learn how to prepare your club's monthly financial report, the most important club document.

Step Seven: Report your taxes to Revenue Canada. Yes, one of life's two certainties — death is the other one — cannot be escaped even in something as innocuous as an investment club. Each club member must declare taxes every year on their income tax returns. Knowing how to calculate each member's tax liability and complete the forms, samples of which are included, can all be found in second last section of the book.

Step Eight: Conduct a year-end assessment. Get back to brass tacks and assess how well your club has met its objectives as set out in step one. Experience shows that only clubs that keep focussed on the learning needs of their members survive over the long-term.

There you have it — eight steps to building a successful investment club. Of course, the devil is in the details, but there is fortunately a lot of detail set out in the next 170 or so pages. You can read them all at once, or you can refer to individual sections as they become relevant to your club. You can also use the detailed index to find information about a particular topic.

Everything you need to get started is here. So what are you waiting for?

Let the fun and learning begin!

HOW TO *start & run*

Contents

an Investment Club
for fun & learning

Section 5 — Setting Up A Flexible Accounting System

Section 6 — Keeping Track Of The Finances

Section 7 — Reporting For Revenue Canada

Section 8 — Investment Club Resources

Why Form An Investment Club?

Fun, learning and, of course, profit are just some of the many benefits of starting your own club.

Notes (Use this space to make notes for your future reference.)

Just what is an investment club?

Investment clubs — usually groups of 10 to 35 people who join together for fun, education and profit — started in Texas more than 90 years ago. Today, there are more than 30,000 investment clubs in the United States. In Canada, the first known investment club began in 1928 when a group of Oshawa schoolteachers formed the Old Canada Investment Club. Today, it is believed that between 3,000 and 5,000 such organizations are operating in Canada — and the number is continuing to grow.

The concept is relatively simple. A group of individuals commits to regular get-togethers (usually monthly) and contributes a set amount (typically about $50) which is jointly invested in investments of the club's choosing.

CHAPTER 1

In some ways, the resulting pool of investments resembles a tiny mutual fund. However, this fund is managed by the club's members, with or without assistance of a professional investment advisor, depending on the club's collective level of expertise. Most clubs conduct their own research but rely on a professional advisor to help them access information and verify their findings.

With typical monthly dues ranging from $25 to $75, investment clubs do not represent, in themselves, a sure-fire road to riches. Rather, they are an entertaining, educational and often profitable way for you to learn how to invest. This is not to say that over a long period of time, contributions to an investment club cannot be substantial. They can play a large role in improving your life, whether it's helping to pay for the kids' education, paying off the mortgage sooner, or contributing to a more comfortable retirement. However, the primary benefit of joining an investment club is that it will help you learn how to improve the performance of all your other investments, too.

Hot Tip

Make learning the primary reason for starting or joining an investment club. Clubs with a strong educational component have a much stronger chance of succeeding over the long-term.

A fun, low-cost way to learn and prosper

Now, you may be asking: "Why go to all that trouble when you can pay a professional mutual fund manager a relatively small fee to do all the work for you?" The answer can be described in three little words: fun, education, and profit.

Make some money

Let's start with the last reason first, which is really the least important. Some people are afraid to entrust their savings to their own judgment or that of their friends when the expert advice of mutual fund managers or investment advisors is available. Well here's a fact that will surprise you:

Doing your own research saves you money and can boost your returns.

In the 1980s, more than 60% of U.S.-based investment clubs outperformed the Standard & Poor's 500 composite index. By comparison, less than 25% of mutual funds were able to beat the S&P. Equivalent comparisons for Canada aren't readily available, but we strongly suspect they would reveal a similar pattern.

So how is it possible that you and your friends on Main Street can consistently beat the performance of those highly paid investment gurus on Bay Street and Wall Street?

The fact that you aren't charging for your own advice makes a big difference. How big? Well, let's assume that your investment club achieves a 10% annual rate of return (capital appreciation plus all dividends reinvested) on its investments. To achieve the same net return on a mutual fund with a 2.5% management fee, you'd have to pick one whose managers were able to achieve an annual rate of return of roughly 12.83%.

Clubs not only pool money, but knowledge, too! Teachers, mechanics and nurses all have "inside" information about their industry. Use it to pick stocks.

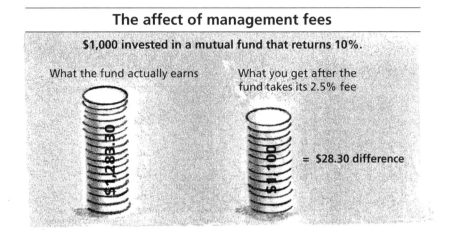

The affect of management fees

$1,000 invested in a mutual fund that returns 10%.

What the fund actually earns

What you get after the fund takes its 2.5% fee

$1,283.30

$1,100

= $28.30 difference

The second reason your judgment counts for more than you might think is that you are living in the real world. While the high finance takes place in Toronto, New York and other money centres, often the earliest signs of a good idea's success, or the promise of a new retailing format, are witnessed first by the everyday consumers upon whose acceptance they will depend. Club members can also know a lot about specific companies or industries.

This isn't to suggest that expert research doesn't play a major role in guiding investment decisions. In fact, learning how to conduct research is one of the main reasons for joining an investment club in the first place. However, it's worth remembering that the gut feel for the potential of an innovative product or service is an important advantage to the small investor. Remember, too, that the collective wisdom of 10 or 20 reasonable people often makes for a better decision than the opinion of a single person, no matter how knowledgeable. Consider, for example, the thousands of home office workers who recognized the enormous potential of Internet technology before it occurred to Microsoft's Bill Gates!

Learn new things

As we've said, picking the right stocks depends on a disciplined approach to research. But as even novice investment club members soon realize, it is a skill that can be learned in a relatively short period of time. That's because – thanks to their team approach – investment clubs share the responsibility for research and member education among several people.

As part of a team, you also have better access to information. Through investment clubs, members can share the cost of what would otherwise be prohibitively expensive investor information services. Best of all, the research and analytical skills you develop through the investment club are yours to keep. Everything you learn in the investment club can be used to help build wealth in your own investment portfolio.

Hot Tip

Being part of an investment club will give you cheaper access to investment research and educational tools because you will often qualify for group discounts.

Have some fun

Perhaps the most important reason for joining an investment club is the fact that meeting with friends to learn how to make money on your investments is a great deal of fun. It's two types of fun really.

First, there's the kind of fun that comes from seeing something you learn really pay off. It's a kind of satisfaction you can't get from lucking out on a hot stock tip or picking the right mutual fund (although neither situation is a painfully disappointing experience).

The other kind of fun – the one which many reports have shown is far and away the most important benefit of joining an investment club – is the camaraderie and sense of mutual accomplishment that comes from getting together with friends for an enjoyable night out, while working in pursuit of a common goal.

In fact, it's not unheard of for clubs to last for 20 or more years and for members to pass on their interest in a club to their children. While such instances are rare to be sure, they serve to show how life-enhancing membership of a successful club can be.

The advantages of an investment club   CHAPTER 2

There are numerous advantages to joining an investment club. Here are some of the main ones:

It doesn't cost much to get started

Most investment clubs are formed by people who have less than $100 a month to invest. In fact, many clubs are formed by people who contribute $25 a month. The average contribution is about $50.

Lower risk

By pooling your contributions with those of your fellow members, you can buy a wider selection of securities. That means you can avoid the kind of risk that comes from "placing

How dollar-cost averaging lowers your cost per share

Investor A Buys $750 worth of ABC stock each month for 6 months

Month	1	2	3	4	5	6	TOTALS	
ABC share price	$10	$7.85	$11.50	$9.90	$13	$8.50		
Shares bought	75	95	65	75	57	88	455 shares	**= $9.83 per share**
Cost	$750	$745.75	$747.50	$742.50	$741	$748	$4,474.75	

Investor B Buys $4,500 worth of ABC in month 1

Month	1	2	3	4	5	6	TOTALS	
ABC share price	$10	-	-	-	-	-		
Shares bought	450	-	-	-	-	-	450 shares	**= $10.00 per share**
Cost	$4,500	-	-	-	-	-	$4,500	

all your eggs in one basket." With a contribution of $50 a month, it would be impossible to create any reasonable measure of diversification on your own, with the exception of a mutual fund investment. But by pooling your $50 contribution with those of 14 other members, for example, you are creating a monthly investment contribution of $750 which means you can start building a diversified portfolio within a few months.

You can get great value for money buying shares through a broker that charges a flat fee for trades under a certain dollar amount eg. $25 for trades under $3,000.

Lower costs

Members of investment clubs benefit from lower costs in a number of ways. One advantage, which applies to any type of regular investment program, is the benefit of dollar cost averaging. Dollar cost averaging is an investment technique where the club spends a set amount on regularly scheduled purchases of a particular stock (or a set of stocks) – whether the market is up or down. By investing the same amount of money each month, you automatically buy more shares when the price is low, and fewer shares when the price is high. As a result, you will find that the average price you pay per share is less than the average price of the stock for a given period of time. The chart above shows how dollar cost averaging can be better than investing one lump sum.

As a member of an investment club, you will also enjoy savings due to lower average commissions. Brokerage firms charge commissions based on a sliding scale, that includes a minimum commission amount for all small orders. This means it's more economical to buy larger amounts of shares, as the table below shows. So the cost of buying or selling a small number of shares on your own can sometimes be prohibitive. When you pool your money with other club members, however, you can afford to buy more shares, thus lowering the commission cost per share.

Commission Savings

The cost of buying ABC stock at $5 per share by yourself or in a club.

	By yourself	In a club of 15 members
Cash available:	$50	$750
Commission:	$25	$ 25
Buying power:	$25	$725
Shares @ $5 each:	5	145
Cost per share:	$50 ÷ 5 shares	$750 ÷ 145 shares
	= $10 each	= $5.17 each
		a savings of 48%!

Easier access to professional advice

Ultimately, brokers or investment advisors (IAs) earn their living based on the quality of their advice. But on a day-to-day basis, their remuneration depends on the value of securities they trade on behalf of their clients. Whereas an individual investment of $50 wouldn't warrant the attention of a professional investment advisor (or go much farther than paying the commission), 15 times that amount on a regular basis is worth the attention of many investment advisors. In fact, some investment advisors even specialize in helping investment clubs.

Opportunities to learn

With the guidance of more experienced investors, and the advice of professional investment advisors, investment clubs

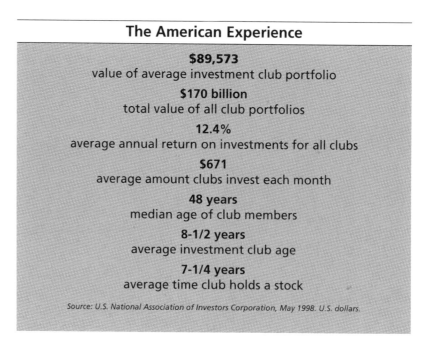

The American Experience

$89,573
value of average investment club portfolio

$170 billion
total value of all club portfolios

12.4%
average annual return on investments for all clubs

$671
average amount clubs invest each month

48 years
median age of club members

8-1/2 years
average investment club age

7-1/4 years
average time club holds a stock

Source: U.S. National Association of Investors Corporation, May 1998. U.S. dollars.

Clubs are a fun, low-cost way to learn.

represent a relatively low-risk, low-cost way to learn about investments as you go.

A rewarding social experience

Advancing your investment knowledge and making money are rewarding pursuits in their own right. But finding a way to do it in the company of friends is a special evening out that most club members look forward to.

Personal satisfaction

A lucky stock pick is definitely not too hard to take. Nor is a passive investment in a top-performing mutual fund. But neither experience comes close to the satisfaction you get from researching the potential of an individual company stock, buying it at an opportune time and, finally, watch what you have learned literally pay off.

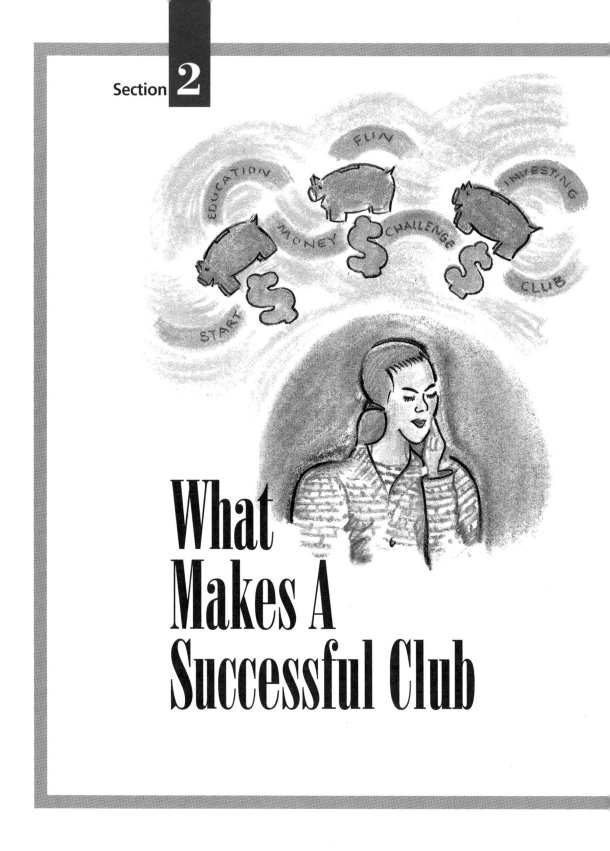

What Makes A Successful Club

Tried and tested steps to help you start an investment club that lasts.

(Use this space to make notes for your future reference.)

Ingredients for a successful club

We've seen that investment clubs offer members a number of compelling benefits.

Yet before you set out to start your own club, it's wise to consider a very sobering fact: despite their obvious benefits and good intentions, 40% of all clubs terminate in the first two years of their existence. Sometimes, it's because a club really has lived up to its mandate of helping members learn how to become successful investors on their own. But all too often, investment clubs fold prematurely because they don't establish goals.

CHAPTER 3

Establish club goals

Now we don't pretend to have a sure-fire recipe for longevity. No two investors are exactly alike and every investment club will reflect the interests and temperaments of its members. But the longest-running and most successful clubs always manage to remember the importance of three basic ingredients in their recipes for success: learning new things, having fun and making money.

While all three are important, ongoing education is the key. Most people like the idea of making a bit of money, especially in the company of friends. But time is an increasingly precious commodity in today's world. A totally satisfying experience requires that people also feel that their time is well spent. In other words, that they are improving themselves by learning a new skill or capability. A healthy investment club ensures its own success by helping people do just that.

By carefully matching the needs of novice investors with the experience of veteran members, by emphasizing investment research, and by keeping the club focused on a

Hot Tip

Spread the work around. Have one member learn some aspect about investing and then teach it to the entire club at the next meeting.

Education, enjoyment and financial enrichment are three key club goals.

monthly investment presentation, the best clubs make sure that something new is learned at every meeting.

Consider your investment approach

As we said, no two investors are alike. So no single investment approach is going to appeal to everyone. But if you are looking for one which has been proven to work for most investors over an extended period of time, no investment approach works better than this one:

Invest regularly.

Novice investors can sometimes be a bit nervous about the timing of their investments. What if, for example, the market takes a dive the day after your club has made its first stock selection? While it's true that the market has its ups and downs, it's reassuring to know that the average annual compound rate of return on stocks has been more than 10% over the last 30 years. So while no one can time short-term fluctuations with certainty, it doesn't really matter when you start to invest. The only important thing is that you invest regularly. And, of course, investing regularly lets you harness the significant benefits of dollar cost averaging.

Reinvest your dividends.

The most successful clubs are also committed to the long-term through dividend reinvestment. This allows them to maximize profits through compounding by plowing all dividends earned back into their investments. Companies generally pay dividends every three months. These might be small sums of money that you might want to let accumulate before you buy more of the company's stock. Your bigger purchase will save you commission dollars per share.

Hot Tip

Your club goals and investment approach can be combined to form a mission statement that you can use to recruit members for your club, and also keep your club on track once it's operating.

Buy and hold for the long-term.

Investing for the long-term is also important. There are many approaches to investing in stocks, but all are overridden by the simple fact that stocks as a whole tend to outperform other investments over the long haul. One approach is to seek out stocks of companies that may be undervalued compared with their peers. This requires detailed research and comparisons with other companies in the same industry.

Another approach is to find so-called growth companies. These are simply those whose sales and earnings are expected to grow faster than the economy at large. Once you've selected a growth company, it makes sense to stick with it only as long as the company continues to meet your expectations.

Speculators who try to forecast short-term market fluctuations, and time their buy and sell decisions accordingly, are bound to be disappointed in the long run. If your club is made up of long-term investors and speculative traders, it's headed for trouble out of the gate. That's why it's important to agree on a long-term investment philosophy before you get started.

Diversify to reduce risk.

Finally, no matter how successful your club might be, some stock picks will be winners, while others will fail to live up to expectations. That's why it makes sense to diversify. The better you diversify your assets, the more you reduce the effect under-performers will have on the overall rate of return of your portfolio.

It's important for members to share the same philosophy.

Select like-minded members

Once you have a clear idea of the club's purpose and investment approach, it's important to seek out potential members
with a similar philosophy. And make sure all members have
approximately the same tolerance for risk. Investing in
precious metal futures, for example, is a far riskier proposition
than placing your money in Canada Savings Bonds.
Discussing your investment temperaments in advance greatly
increases the chances the club will be able to make investment decisions that will keep everyone interested without
causing any members to lose sleep. As we mention later on,
it's a good idea to arrange an informal "pre-mix" meeting to
get people thinking about what they want to get out of the
club.

Make sure
everyone buys
into a long-term
investing philos-
ophy for the club.

If there's one thing you most want in a fellow member it's a sense of responsibility to make the club work. You want people who are as interested in investing as you are, and who are willing to carry their fair share of the club's workload.

A variety of backgrounds is best

Friends and relatives are obvious candidates for your club. So are fellow workers. You can also meet investors by enrolling in an educational investment seminar. Many good friendships have sprung between people who've taken the Investor Learning Centre's national seminar program Intelligent Investing, which is available in a large number of locations across Canada.

A useful tool for recruiting founding members is a club recruitment kit. This should be given to prospective members either at or before your informal pre-mix meeting. It should include a number of key pieces of information:

• An invitation to your informal meeting;

• A statement from you about your reasons for wanting to start the club and what you envisage will be the club's mission, i.e. to learn about investing in solid blue-chip stocks. Also outline briefly what time and money commitment will be expected of the potential member;

• A copy of a sample club constitution (see page 152);

• Names of other interested people; and,

• Investment questionnaire (see page 150).

A quick way to recruit founding members for your club is to ask three friends to each bring two other interested people. If you do the same, you'll have 12 potential members to start with.

People of different backgrounds add depth of experience to your club.

But no matter where your fellow club members come from, try to maintain a healthy degree of diversity in their work backgrounds and life experiences. Whether you are considering an investment in a bank, a computer technology firm, a retail food chain or any other company, having members from various walks of life can help provide different and valuable perspectives on a single industry.

If there is one occupational background that's welcome at any club, it's that of a bookkeeper or accountant. Most investment club accounting is quite straightforward. And there are standard record-keeping forms and various computer programs that can make the job easier, including some at the back of this book. Still, if your club is lucky enough to include a member who is familiar with accounting, you are ahead of the game. An accountant is ideal, since they also can handle tax reporting at year end.

On the other hand, some clubs purposely avoid having a resident financial expert. The concern is that their presence will cause other members to defer responsibility for making decisions, thus defeating the team-based learning approach that the club has been established to promote. Besides, most clubs operate quite well without an accountant in their ranks, although many use the services of an outside accountant to prepare year-end financial statements and issue individual tax forms.

When considering how much accounting expertise your club needs, try to remember two things. First, the cost of these services varies quite a bit depending on how much of the leg-work you can do yourself . Second, belonging to the club won't be a fun and rewarding experience if you are paying someone else to run the club for you.

And besides, Sections 5, 6 and 7 of this book do a pretty good job explaining how to do basic club accounting. Follow these simple steps and you shouldn't need more than someone to give your records a quick review.

Select the right number of members

What's the right number of members for your investment club? There is no right answer to this question, but 10 to 15 seems to be a nice workable average. That number will give you a sufficient "pool" from which to assign and rotate responsibilities, including the task of tracking individual stocks in which the club is interested. In any event, the upper limit on the size of your club is 50 members. That's the point at which Revenue Canada begins to treat your investment club as a mutual fund.

Hot Tip

The best talker in the club isn't necessarily the best stock-picker. Make sure everyone is involved and feels comfortable giving an opinion.

Get to know each other

Often, the best way to consider these issues is through an informal gathering of prospective members. This allows people to get acquainted and ensures that everyone is reasonably like-minded about the club's intended purpose and investment approach. It's also a good opportunity to set a time for the club's first formal meeting. To prepare for it, it's often a good idea to distribute informal investment questionnaires. These will help ensure that members have a clearer idea of their own investment goals at the club's first meeting. You should collect the questionnaires and prepare a summary for your first formal meeting. A sample questionnaire is included at the back of this book (see page 150). Additional materials, such as a sample club constitution (see page 152), or copies of this book, will also be helpful.

Develop a phone list of members at your pre-mix session. You can call to remind them of the first meeting and also hear their thoughts about the club.

The First Meeting

How to get your investment club
up and running on a solid footing.

Notes (Use this space to make notes for your future reference.)

The fun and learning starts

CHAPTER 4

You've had your informal pre-mix session and time has come for your first formal meeting.

You've got 15 enthusiastic people together in your living room. The energy is electric and the noise level deafening. How are you going to get anything done tonight?

This is the kind of happy chaos that greets almost all clubs on their first night together. The risk is you won't achieve much at the first meeting, which is bound to leave more than a few members doubting the club's viability right out of the starting gate.

As with all your meetings, you can get them on track by preparing an agenda. For the first meeting, hand out copies to people as they arrive. For subsequent meetings it's a good idea to make sure everyone gets an agenda a few days ahead of time. This gives people a chance to prepare, which in turn speeds up the club's more mundane proceedings.

Since there's a lot to get through at the first meeting, it's a good idea to set a time limit for each agenda item. Any issues that aren't resolved in that time can be held over to the next meeting. This way you'll get through the agenda and people will feel you've made progress.

Since the meeting is being held at your place, you should probably chair the first meeting. Later on, probably at your next meeting, you'll be electing from out of the group a club president who will chair most future meetings. As well, you'll want to have someone take minutes of the key points discussed. These notes needn't be detailed, but they should capture major decisions by the majority of club members. Keeping club minutes will become the job of the club secretary.

Stick to the agenda to stay on track. When in doubt, vote.

The minutes from the first and subsequent meetings will be helpful in drawing up your club's constitution. You'll want to have all members agree to a draft constitution by the end of your third or fourth meeting. You'll find a sample constitution on page 152. Let it serve as a guideline for the kinds of topics you need to agree on, but change it to suit your club's specific needs.

Don't rush the constitution, but also don't let it consume too much of your club's time. After all, your club is about learning to pick investments — so that's what should get most of your time.

Okay, let's take a look now at the things you'll want to cover at the first meeting. You can use the points that follow as the basis for your own agenda.

Re-affirm the club's goals and purpose

All of that pre-planning should be enough to keep you from assembling a mix of international currency speculators and GIC investors at the first meeting. Still, it would be a good idea to start the evening by reaffirming the club's general purpose and investment philosophy. If you've already distributed investment questionnaires and other information materials, this is a good time to summarize results and openly discuss any divergence of opinion.

Develop a standard agenda that you can use for each meeting, rather than developing a new agenda each time.

Choose a structure

There are two ways to structure your investment club: the easy way and the more difficult way. The more difficult way is to formally set up a company, either a corporation or a partnership. This involves extra costs, more legwork, and — you guessed it – dealing with government bureaucracy.

Investment clubs that are set up as corporations are subject to two types of taxation: the club must pay corporate level income tax on its earnings and the individual members must pay tax on income received in the form of dividends from the club.

Some clubs register themselves as businesses called partnerships. This involves filling out forms, doing a name search through a paralegal firm and paying registration fees. If you choose to become a formal partnership, you'll likely also need to consult a lawyer about drafting a formal partnership agreement. Partnerships are taxed differently than corporations. Any income tax is paid by the partners and not by the partnership itself.

Hot Tip

The sample constitution on page 152 includes a bylaw about the modified partnership. By having all members sign it, you will have set up your own modified partnership.

There may be times when this more complex structure makes sense, but it's unnecessary in most cases. That's because Revenue Canada allows investment clubs to adopt a far simpler structure called a 'modified partnership.' This is almost exactly like a formal partnership except that you don't have to register it.

In fact, all you have to do to become a modified partnership is agree to become one. Once everyone agrees, you send a letter to Revenue Canada signed by all the members. This means Revenue Canada won't subject your club itself to tax. Instead, each club member is simply responsible for reporting their share of the club's income on their individual tax returns each year.

To qualify for tax treatment as a modified partnership, your club must meet all of the following conditions:

a) All of the club's members must be individuals;

b) Most members cannot come from the same family;

c) Members of the same family cannot own more than half of the club's assets;

d) Most of the club's property must consist of cash, shares, bonds, or units of a mutual fund; and,

e) Sales of club assets will give rise to capital gains or losses rather than gains or losses in income.

The modified partnership structure is easy to set up.

The modified partnership requires that you keep records of each member's adjusted cost base. This is an accounting measurement that simply calculates how much of your share in the club you must pay tax on. In other words, it helps determine the capital gains and losses that arise when you sell of any of your shares in the club. Page 129 shows you how the adjusted cost base is calculated, as well as related information on Revenue Canada filing requirements.

To be treated as a modified partnership, all you have to do is send a letter to Revenue Canada along with the club's income tax return. The letter should state that the club has agreed to be treated as a modified partnership. All members should sign the letter and each should be given a copy for their records (see sample letter on page 163).

Choosing a name

You can call your club anything you like so long as the name is original. Generally speaking, it's best to choose something that clearly states the club's nature, such as Teachers' Investment Club of Hamilton. It's also important to choose a name that is unlikely to be chosen by another group, or confused with an existing business. Some clubs include the year their club was founded in the name — such as Teachers' Investment Club of Hamilton 1998 — to be even clearer.

Setting dues

Although there's no law against allowing members to vary their contributions every month, our advice is to set dues at a fixed amount per person at the beginning. This makes it much easier to keep track of the finances. If later you want to let people contribute differing amounts, or if you want to admit new members, you will still be able to do so with only minor adjustment to how you keep track of the club's money.

Setting fixed dues also means all members have an equal share in the club's assets. This can have a profound effect on the nature and psychological dynamics of the club. If the club's purpose is to have fun while you are learning, an equal contribution between members is probably best. That way, everyone has the same stake in the club's decisions, which makes it easier to maintain the club's democratic spirit.

Having said all that, some clubs allow members to vary contributions according to personal interest and circumstances. Thanks to a unit system of record keeping the accounting is less trouble than it might seem. The unit system also allows for greater flexibility when members leave the club or when new members join. However, you don't have to start with the unit system right off the bat. You can start with fixed dues and then change to a unit system if the need arises. See Section 5 for guidance on setting up a unit accounting system.

The second consideration is the amount of the monthly dues. Again, there is no single amount that is right for every club, but the figure would seem to average about $50. Remember, there should be enough at stake to keep the experience interesting, but not so much that it becomes a burden for any of the members. It also should not represent any member's primary source of investment or retirement savings. In fact, investment clubs usually represent a small fraction of a member's overall investment portfolio. That's the way it should be because investment clubs are designed to be a low-risk way of learning about investments as you go.

The amount of dues should let you operate the club economically. This will depend on a number of factors, including the number of people in your club. If you have 15

No member should be allowed to own more than 20% of the club's total assets. This will curb the amount of influence any single member can have.

Make dues collection a permanent item on the club's agenda. That way, no one can claim they forgot.

members, a monthly investment of $50 will give you $750. You will also want to make investments often enough to keep things interesting. If your target investment frequency is an average of once every two months, that means you'll have $1,500 to invest in each investment period. You'll probably want to buy and sell your securities in board lots (usually batches of 100) to get the best price for them, so the dues should give you enough to do this.

Another payment to consider is an annual administration fee. This amount — usually about $25 to $50 per member per year — goes towards covering the costs of running the club. It's kept in the club's chequing account and is used for the costs of accounting services, postage, stationery, and other miscellaneous expenses. The administration fee is usually levied once per year, generally on the anniversary of the club's founding. When a new member joins, they should pay this fee along with their first month's dues.

Of course, since your club doesn't yet have a bank account, you won't be collecting cheques at the first meeting. The administration fee, plus the first month's dues, should be paid at the club's next meeting, which is when you will be completing the forms to open a bank account.

Opening a bank account

One of the first things you'll have to do is find a safe place to put the club's money. Most banks have special accounts for investment clubs and can provide you with all the information you need to set one up. Funds on deposit in the account are usually withdrawn by cheques signed by two members chosen by the club. Assign a member now to obtain forms and account details from a bank for the next meeting. Since you'll be electing club officials at that meeting, you'll have a clearer idea of who should have signing power on the account. One of those people will be whoever is elected club treasurer. The bank account is really only used to deposit members' monthly dues before transferring them to the club's brokerage firm. It also holds funds for the clubs annual administrative expenses.

Selecting a brokerage

Any club that is going to buy and sell stocks is going to need the services of an investment or brokerage firm. Basically, there are two types: discount and full-service. The discount broker offers lower commissions on trades but generally speaking provides nothing in the way of advice. Some discount brokers offer free research and educational tools to clients.

Full-service brokerages charge somewhat higher commissions but their service includes advice on individual securities and access to information from the firm's research department. This extra service may, or may not, be worth the money to you depending on the extent to which the club will be doing its own research.

Hot Tip

Many discount brokerages have Internet trading sites. All members can get access to the club's account information and up-to-date valuations on the club's portfolio 24 hours a day.

The amount of the club's assets can also play a part in your decision. The bigger your club's portfolio gets, the more attention you'll likely get from a full-service investment advisor (IA). That doesn't mean you must have a lot of money before going to a full-service firm. On the contrary, most full-service firms welcome all new business because they see it as an opportunity to show 15 people the value of their services. From their perspective, if club members are happy with the firm's services, chances are they'll open individual accounts with the firm. Most full-service firms can also provide advice on how to run a club properly.

If your club's decision is to use a full-service IA, it makes sense to interview several of them to ensure that you select one whose investment approach is compatible with your club's needs. If you plan to employ a "buy and hold" strategy, it doesn't make sense to select an IA who likes to trade frequently based on short-term prospects or the ups and downs of the economy.

That said, the right IA can be an invaluable source of investment advice and a critical ally in helping to realize the club's educational goals. Here's a short list of things to consider when you are looking for an IA:

• Get several recommendations from people you trust;

• Interview each candidate to determine their investment approach and make sure they are comfortable working with investment clubs;

• Ask about the IA's experience and any designations they might have;

• Ask for references and be sure to follow them up;

• Ask what kind of services the broker could provide to further the educational mandate of the club; and,

Financial designations — what they mean

Title	Education	Experience
FCSI — Fellow of the Canadian Securities Institute	Minimum 5 securities courses + exams	5+ years
CFA — Chartered Financial Analyst	Completion of three-part CFA program	3+ years
CIM — Canadian Investment Manager	Completion of the Canadian Investment Management program — 3 courses	no requirement
CFP — Certified Financial Planner	One course and exam	2+ years

• Check that the firm is a member of the Canadian Investor Protection Fund (CIPF), an organization that monitors firms and covers investors if a brokerage goes insolvent, within prescribed limits.

Since this is the first meeting, it's unlikely you'll have had time to interview propective investment firms. Now's a good time to assign several people to research prospective firms and report back at the next meeting.

The report-back should cover things like the firm's commission schedule on a typical trade your club will be doing, and what other services the firm can offer. Once club members have decided on a firm, you'll have to complete an application form, so it's a good idea to bring these to the next meeting.

Hot Tip

Invite a full-service investment advis-or to a meeting. Interview them to see if they fit with the club's objectives.

Nominating club officials

An investment club cannot operate efficiently unless individual members take on specific responsibilities. Although you probably won't have time to consider candidates and elect officials at the first meeting, it's a good idea to circulate a description of the duties for each position and ask members to give consideration to likely candidates.

Officers should be democratically elected by club members for a specified length of time. Most clubs choose a term of one year and hold elections annually for most positions, but longer terms are not uncommon. This is especially true for the position of treasurer. Typically, it involves a greater amount of work and expertise than the other positions. So members who are good at keeping track of the numbers are often prevailed upon to keep doing it.

The first step in the election process is to create a nominating committee. You can do this at the first meeting. Once formed, it's this committee's responsibility to:

• Ask each member of the club to recommend candidates for each position;

• Develop a list of suitable candidates for each position;

• Speak to each member of the club privately to determine if they would like to run for a particular position; and,

• Present the membership with a slate of candidates for all positions at the club's next meeting.

Most clubs hold a democratic election by secret ballot at their second meeting. If a member can't attend the election, provision is usually made for another member to vote on his or her behalf by proxy.

Listed below are brief descriptions of the duties and responsibilities of the elected positions commonly found in investment clubs:

President: The president appoints committees, oversees the activities of the club and sets the time, place and chairs all club meetings.

Vice-President: The vice-president takes on the responsibilities of the president when the president is absent. He or she is also responsible for organizing the educational content of the meeting, which usually takes the form of a 10– to 15– minute presentation. The vice-president is also responsible for arranging guest speakers and field trips.

Secretary: The secretary is responsible for keeping a record of all that transpires at the meeting in the form of minutes. At the beginning of every meeting, the secretary reads the minutes of the previous meeting and makes any required corrections. Minutes are then approved by a vote and entered into the permanent record.

Treasurer: The treasurer maintains all of the club's financial records, issues all buy and sell orders to the broker, and prepares monthly statements of financial transactions as well as each member's interest in the club. In addition, the treasurer is responsible for preparing the annual tax information for each member.

The treasurer is also responsible for delegating research on prospective investments to individual members.

Attention to detail and a basic familiarity with book-keeping are welcome attributes in this important job. If you don't have a member who's an accountant by day, the treasurer

Try to get as many people involved as possible. Why not have a research director, an assistant treasurer or a social director?

Meetings held in the second half of the month allow your treasurer more time to prepare the club's monthly financial report with data from the latest brokerage statement.

can do most of the routine record keeping and rely on professional assistance to audit the books and prepare tax statements once a year.

Reviewing the club's constitution

Once you've given consideration to all of these subjects, you are probably ready to have a look at a draft constitution. While investment clubs are supposed to be fun, they are also in the very serious business of handling people's money. That's why a formal constitution is a must.

Simply put, the constitution is the rule book that governs what the club — and its members — can and cannot do, and how it goes about its business. The constitution formalizes every aspect of the club's operation including:

- The club's purpose and investment strategy;

- The size and frequency of dues;

- Voting procedures;

- The election and responsibilities of club officials; and,

- What happens when someone leaves the club.

A sample constitution has been included on page 152 to help get you started. There's likely to be much discussion around the constitution, but try to limit the amount of time spent on it to avoid getting bogged down in details. It's a good idea to have one member draw up a draft constitution. This should be circulated to all members and discussed briefly at your next meeting.

By the third meeting, you should have enough input from members to start drafting your final constitution for each

Hot Tip

Adopt the sample constitution at the back of this book as your interim constitution until you've had time to consider your own final constitution.

member's approval. It might also be a good idea to consult a lawyer to make sure it's clearly and precisely worded before it is formally adopted. But even then, don't expect your constitution to be foolproof. Circumstances will arise from time to time that require the constitution to be amended or enhanced.

The longer your club exists, the more goodwill and camaraderie is built between members. Pretty soon you'll be enjoying the social and investment aspects of the club so much that the constitution will seem unimportant. However, if the need ever arises for a difficult decision to be made, you'll have the constitution to refer to.

Choosing a time and place to meet

This sounds like a simple task but remember, the smooth functioning of your club depends on the regular attendance of as many members as possible. Try to pick a day and time that works well for everyone at the outset.

Meetings at members' homes are fraught with interruptions like phone calls. If your club is serious about its business, consider meeting on more neutral turf.

Choosing where to meet every month obviously depends on where members live. A single, central location — like a church basement — works best for some clubs. Probably the most popular option is to rotate the meeting from one member's house to another. Most often, responsibility for food and beverages goes with it. If you choose this arrangement, make sure to distribute a location schedule several months in advance.

Choosing a regular time to meet is also important. It's best to choose a date that members will remember, such as the third Tuesday of every month at 7:00 p.m., or the very next business day if one of those Tuesdays falls on a holiday.

How To
Keep Your
Club Running
Smoothly

Notes (Use this space to make notes for your future reference.)

Conducting productive meetings

Once you manage to get through the business of the first meeting, conducting the ongoing affairs of the club should be fairly easy by comparison.

As in anything else, success comes more easily to those who are organized. This section explains how to conduct productive meetings, how to make an effective presentation of a potential new investment, and how to create committees to help with the smooth running of the club's affairs.

Perhaps the most basic rule about running a productive meeting is that it should always be centred around an agenda. An agenda will give you a "track to run on" and help keep the meeting focused.

CHAPTER 5

A carefully considered agenda will help you make sure that meetings are efficient, informative and entertaining. A well-planned meeting need not last more than 90 minutes and all members should be left with the impression that their time was well spent.

The club secretary is responsible for drafting the agenda and for sending copies of it, along with the minutes from the last meeting, to each member a week before the meeting. Getting the agenda and minutes in the mail, or by e-mail, will remind members of the next meeting. It also gives everyone the chance to review the minutes for quick approval at the meeting.

Here's a basic outline of a typical investment club agenda:

Call the meeting to order

The president — who acts as chair of the meeting — is responsible for calling the meeting to order. Start the meeting promptly out of respect to those members who showed up on time and to make a point to those who didn't.

Read and approve of the minutes

The secretary is responsible for reading the minutes recorded at the last meeting. He or she should then ask members if there are any corrections or additions. Once the minutes are agreed upon, they should be approved with a show of hands.

Minutes can be as brief as you want provided they cover all the important business of the meeting. This would include all motions, amendments, and buy and sell decisions.

Collect club dues

This item is always on the agenda, lest anyone forget that there are dues to pay for the privilege of belonging to your club.

Present the financial report

Responsibility for reviewing the club's financial position rests with the treasurer. The review should include any bank and brokerage account balances, the current value of the club's portfolio and each member's share of it. More information about the financial report and keeping track of the club's finances is contained in Section 6 on page 94.

Review the current holdings

During the financial report, the treasurer will have provided information about the value of each holding from the club's most recent brokerage account statement. However, this part of the meeting is where club members discuss each holding in greater detail and consider more current information. Each member is responsible for keeping track of one or two investments and reporting on them at the meeting.

The report on each holding should begin with an updated price for the stock from the day's newspaper. The stock's most recent price/earnings ratio and dividend yield should be mentioned. The member should then discuss any recent developments surrounding the company. Has anything happened over the past month that could affect the company's earnings? Has there been any news about the company in the papers? Are the company's quarterly operating results available?

It's a good idea for each member to compile a report on each stock on a standard sheet that everyone else uses, too. News releases, articles, quarterly reports and any other information should be attached to the sheet and copies made for all members. See the sample standard stock review sheet on page 54.

Hot Tip

For stocks that you're responsible for tracking, call the companies directly and ask them to put you on their quarterly report mailing list.

ILC Investment Club

01 / 12 / 99

Monthly Stock Review Sheet

Security: _XYZ Co._

Stock exchange: _TSE_   **Shares held:** _100_

Recent price: _$32_   **52 week Hi/Lo:** _$19 – $33.35_

Adjusted Cost Base*: _$20.31_

Dividend Yield†: _0.3%_   **P/E†:** _22_

Target sell P/E†: _30_   **Stop loss:** _$25_

Recent news: _XYZ jumped $4.50 in past month because of 48% increase in earnings in 2nd Quarter. Announced last week, it has won two contracts to build rail cars for Brazil, value $200 million. Sales forecast to increase 35%. EPS† expected to increase 40%. Annual sales projected to increase 35%. EPS expected to increase 40%._

My recommendation: _Hold. Increase stop loss to $30._

Club's decision: _15_ voted to hold.

_–_ voted to sell _–_ shares @ $ _–_

_–_ voted to buy _–_ shares @ $ _–_

_15_ voted to increase/decrease
stop loss to $ _30_

*see Section 7 on page 128.

† see pages 61 - 62 for definitions.

At the end of each company review, members must decide whether to hold, sell or add to each investment. When two-thirds of the members vote to buy or sell a security, the treasurer is directed to arrange the necessary trades, normally within 24 hours.

New investments

Occasionally, the club needs to make new investments with money from new member contributions, accumulated dues, dividends, or from the sale of previous investments. Picking the right investment takes time, open discussion and above all, plenty of research. Often, the club will identify investment opportunities during the meeting and ask one of the members to present a more detailed analysis at the next meeting.

Do a thorough annual review of each stock you own when the companies new annual report is released. Is its growth still on target? Might you buy more or sell?

If someone has been tasked at the last meeting with researching a particular company, this is the time for them to make their presentation to the members. Chapter 6 on page 59 contains information designed to help you make a presentation on a potential new stock investment.

Many times, members won't be ready to make a decision about a potential investment immediately after the member's presentation. A decision can be held over to the next meeting to give members time to review what has been presented.

If a decision has been held over from a previous meeting, it's a good idea to deal with the matter after hearing the latest presentation. That way members will have the benefit of additional context on whether to invest in the stock presented at the last meeting. You might decide on hearing about this latest stock that it is a better investment for the club's money.

A decision on whether to invest in a particular stock should be done by a vote of all members present. Most clubs require a vote of two-thirds of members for any proposal to be carried.

If the decision is in favor of buying the stock, it will need to be determined how many shares to buy, at what price and who is to be responsible for ongoing monitoring of the stock. Usually, ongoing monitoring rests with the person who made the presentation.

Many clubs, recognizing the limitations of meeting only once per month, use a form of insurance called a stop loss order. A stop loss order can limit your losses or protect your gains on a stock investment.

If you have just bought a stock you can use the stop loss order to limit your losses should the stock drop sharply in value. If the stock price rises you can adjust the stop loss order to a higher value to lock in your profits (see page 64).

It's important to keep close track of your stop loss orders to avoid them being triggered when it doesn't suit you.

Educational presentation

Once the club's core business has been finished, it's time for the educational component of the meeting. Usually, it consists of a 15-minute presentation or discussion on the types or principles of investment. To keep things interesting, most clubs will occasionally invite guest speakers – such as bankers, investment analysts, accountants and other professionals – to address the group or lead the discussion. Organizing the educational component of the meeting is the vice-president's responsibility, with help and suggestions from the education committee.

Hot Tip

Pick an industry to study and assign specific stocks for people to research for the next meeting. This will let you compare companies in the same sector.

A good educational component will hold member interest in the club.

Action items

At this point, partners are assigned specific responsibilities for future meetings. The treasurer might be directed to make a particular trade or the vice-president might be directed to ask for the broker's help in setting up an educational presentation on a specific investment topic. A time and place for the next meeting should also be confirmed.

Hot Tip

Send one or two club members to a workshop or educational program and have them come back and teach the entire club what they learned.

Adjournment

After asking whether there are any other items members might want to discuss, the president adjourns the meeting.

With any luck, your meeting has successfully been fitted into the 90 minutes allotted to it. It's the president's job to ensure meetings keep on track. But that doesn't mean club meetings should be rigid and formal. The president should allow time for discussion. Perhaps a member has just finished reading a good book about investing and wants to share a review of it with other members. Or maybe there's an interesting seminar or investment show which members might want to attend.

Also, from time to time there will be other important issues on the agenda, such as the addition of a new member or the resignation of an existing one. The president — or the vice-president in the president's absence — should always be familiar with what the club's constitution says about such matters and be prepared to lead the discussion.

Making a presentation on a new investment

Similar to most endeavors, your chances of making the right stock selection improve dramatically with a bit of research. In an investment club, each member is usually assigned responsibility for a specific company. This team approach results in the club covering a lot more possibilities than a solitary investor could. By the same token, however, there must be a standardized way of presenting potential investment opportunities for the collective consideration of the club.

An effective stock presentation will contain each of the following elements:

CHAPTER 6

Stock price performance

To assess the market value of an investment, it's always a good idea to start with a recent history of the target company's stock price performance. You should include such things as the current stock price, high and low stock prices for the past 52 weeks, the price to earnings (P/E) ratio, the average monthly volume of trading in the stock, and the exchanges on which it is traded.

This information is readily available from daily newspapers, the Internet and the investor relations departments of most public companies.

Ask the investor relations department of a company you're interested in to send you any recent analyst research reports on the company. These are often the best sources of information. They can also be obtained from many full-service and discount brokerage firms.

Company profile

Stock prices are important, but it's essential to give fellow members a strong sense of the subject company's business. Your presentation should include details about the company's products and or services, as well as its growth strategies, competitive advantages, primary markets and earnings history. The last piece of information is especially important because companies that have been able to increase their earnings in the past are more likely to keep doing it in the future. All of this information is available through annual reports, broker reports and — in print form or on the Internet — through various stock report services.

News

Stock markets value companies based on a combination of past performance and expectations, which makes news on recent and impending developments continuously important. Be sure that your presentation covers such things as major industry developments, commodity price swings, new stock or debt issues, significant contracts, or evidence of key executives loading up on the company's stock. News sources include business papers and company conference calls and press releases. Several Internet investor services are also capable of tracking all news items related to specific companies.

Financial health

No matter how impressive the company's earnings growth and prospects, you'll also need to make sure that it's in sound financial condition. Here are some examples of the basic measures that will help in your analysis:

Current ratio: a comparison of current assets to current liabilities, this ratio measures the health of the company's balance sheet. It's intended to show a company's ability to pay current obligations from current assets. Generally speaking, a company with small inventory and readily collectible accounts can safely operate with a lower current ratio than a company whose cash flow is less predictable.

Return on equity: calculated by dividing the company's net income by the shareholders' equity, return on equity (ROE) tells investors how effectively their money is being employed. Comparing ROE percentages for current and previous periods is a good way to measure how well a company is performing relative to its competitors.

Earnings per share: the portion of a company's profit allocated to each outstanding share of common stock, earnings per share (EPS) is the ultimate measure of a company's ability to operate profitably.

To learn how to calculate these ratios yourself, study two of them during each of your first few educational sessions of your monthly meetings. Several books are available to assist you in your learning. See Section 8 on page 148 for a list.

Cash flow: Narrowly defined as net income plus depreciation and other non-cash charges, cash flow is an important indicator of a company's ability to pay dividends. In a larger sense, the cash flow statement itemizes all cash that flows into, and out of, the company. If more money flows in than out, it's called a positive cash flow. Even if a company's assets exceed its liabilities, it can still go bankrupt if it cannot generate enough cash to meet current obligations.

Estimated earnings: Based on these and other factors, most brokerage firms — most often with considerable guidance from the companies they are following — issue earnings estimates for the next quarter. Generally speaking, if such estimates are higher than the equivalent quarter in the previous fiscal year, it's a sign that the company is headed in the right direction. If the earnings estimate is lower, it may signal a warning, or perhaps, a buying opportunity.

How to calculate the ratios

Current Ratio $= \dfrac{\text{current assets}}{\text{current liabilities}}$

Return on Equity $= \dfrac{\text{net earnings (before extraordinary items) - preferred dividends}}{\text{common equity}} \times 100$

Earns per Share $= \dfrac{\text{net earnings (before extraordinary items) - preferred dividends}}{\text{number of common shares outstanding}}$

Cash Flow = net earnings (before extraordinary items) - equity income + minority interest in earnings of subsidiaries + deferred income taxes + depreciation + other non-cash charges e.g. depletion, amoritization etc.

Price/Earning Ratio $= \dfrac{\text{current market price of common}}{\text{earnings per share (in latest 12-month period)}}$

Your presentation should measure your subject company in terms of these criteria and also include a comparison to similar companies. The information you need to complete your analysis is readily available through annual reports as well as stock reports such as the Blue Book or The Financial Post Investor Reports (see page 143).

Of course, inexperienced members of the club will have difficulty doing this type of detailed research. They will need to learn how to read an annual report and company financial statements. It's a good idea to make this topic the subject the club's first few educational presentations. If you need to know more about how to calculate and interpret these and other financial indicators, one of our related publications — *How to Read Financial Statements* — will be of valuable assistance. For even more information, you can recommend the book *How to Invest in Canadian Securities.*

Inexperienced members should be paired with more experienced members when assigned to make a stock presentation. This will allow the novice member an opportunity to learn from the experienced member.

Hot Tip

Several news release distribution companies will e-mail you company news releases as soon as they become available. For a list of these, check out the links section of Carlson Online at www. fin-info.com

The recommendation

The ultimate aim of your analysis, of course, is to select a portfolio of well-managed companies with solid track records and excellent prospects for continued growth. So make sure that your presentation ends with a recommendation, even if it's to devote no more time to following a particular stock. When you determine that buying a stock makes sense, try to establish a target purchase price. Some clubs also determine a target sell price in advance, based on historical P/E multiples. They will know from past performance what the stock's high and low P/E range is, and then select in advance a P/E at which they will sell the stock. If the stock's current P/E is 15, and the historical range is between 8 and 25, the club might decide to sell when the P/E reaches 25. This means that regardless of whether the stock price goes up or down, the club will sell when the share price is at the top of its expensive range. Using and sticking by this method, gives the club an objective means of assessing when to sell, rather than one which is clouded by personal sentiment.

Some clubs also take out a stop loss order on a stock when they first buy it. Stop loss orders are useful for clubs since no one individual has the right to sell a club holding. So if one of the club's holdings is rocked by bad news, a decision to sell may have to be delayed for a month until the club meets again. By then, it could be too late. However, a pre-approved stop loss order will automatically kick in when the price falls to the club's sell price. It's important to keep track of the stop loss orders on each holding, and revise their levels from time to time to lock in profits.

The following schedule provides a rule of thumb for setting the price of stop loss orders:

- Speculative stocks: 20% below current price

- Mid-cap stocks: 15% below current price

- Senior blue-chip stocks: 10% below current price

Hot Tip

Make buy and sell decisions as a club and don't look back or finger-point if the decision doesn't pan out as expected.

Creating committees

Most clubs form committees to help elected officers share the workload and make running the club a more educational experience for all members. Each committee should consist of no more than three members. Here's a brief description of the committees most commonly found at investment clubs and what tasks they should perform.

Education committee

This committee aids the vice-president in selecting topics for the educational component of the meeting. Providing members with a continuing education in investments is the key to your club's long-term success. If your club regularly has an interesting educational topic on the agenda, it will encourage members to keep attending.

CHAPTER 7

The education committee's job is to find out from all members what topics are of most interest to them and whether they know of potential guest speakers who could address the club. The committee should keep a list of members' interests and educational needs and try to ensure that these are addressed during the course of each year. They can do this by either assigning one or more members to research and present findings on a particular topic or by finding qualified guests to speak to the club.

Some topics that are always of interest at clubs include:

- How to calculate financial ratios and why they're important;
- Learning how interest rates affect the stock market;
- What bonds are and how they differ from stocks;
- Reviewing investment books and magazines;
- The risks and rewards of buying on margin;
- How to use options for profit and protection; and,
- Buying index participation units.

If each member learns just one new thing at every meeting, they'll feel that their time has been well spent. That'll keep them coming back month after month — and who knows, perhaps even year after year.

Nominating committee

This committee is responsible for developing a slate of qualified candidates for each executive position and for conducting club elections (see page 44).

Audit and investment committee

This committee is comprised of non-officer members who monitor the record keeping function and verify the accuracy of

An annual review of the club's performance is always helpful.

the club's financial records. Members are also responsible for preparing an annual review of the club's investment successes and failures. Questions to consider in this review include:

• Is everyone happy with the way the club is selecting stocks for research?

• Do the current holdings fit with the club's objectives and members' risk profiles?

• Are there any industries or investment categories that the club should take the time to research in the coming year?

By conducting this annual review, you will ensure that your club will continue to meet the needs of its members. Individual members will also feel that they are being given a say in the club's future direction.

To engage people in club respon-sibilities, consider electing deputies for all positions and alter-nating duties every second month with the primary office bearer.

Setting Up A Flexible Accounting System

How the unit value accounting
system helps simplify your
club's finances.

Setting Up A Flexible Accounting System

 (Use this space to make notes for your future reference.)

When to start

In the early stages of your club's growth, you won't have a lot of money to invest. Depending on how many members you have and the level of dues being paid, you probably won't be in a position to make your first investment until your third or fourth month.

Once you start investing, though, it's important to set up an accounting system that members can easily follow. As soon as club money is committed to the fortunes of a particular stock, you can bet that members will be keeping an eager eye on the investment's performance. This is when the club treasurer's role takes on a new level of importance. Members will want an update at each monthly meeting on how their stake in the club is doing.

CHAPTER 8

In fact, making investments is the surest way to grab and sustain member interest in your club. The sooner you can make that first investment the better. Any delay of more than four months or so and you run the risk of members bailing out for lack of interest.

Invest as soon as possible

A big factor to consider here is your club's setup costs. At the start, fees for lawyers, accountants, stationary and other supplies can take a fair chunk out of members' dues. This will hamper your club's ability to start investing early, so it's worth mentioning again that many clubs levy a small annual fee to help defray these costs. At about $25 to $50 per year, the fee is paid by each member with the first month's dues and then again on the club's anniversary or the beginning of each year, whichever is more practical.

With 10 members in your club, you will have $500 a year to cover ongoing administrative costs and professional fees. This money should be deposited in the club's bank account and not with the brokerage firm. It should also be excluded from any calculations of the value of your club's portfolio. As club members gain more experience and become less reliant on professional services, you can reduce the administrative fee.

By paying this administrative fee, you will very soon be in a position to make your club's first investment. If you have 10 members, and each pays monthly dues of $50, you'll have $1,500 available to be invested by your fourth meeting. This is probably enough to buy your first investment. The small act of buying stock in a company should galvanize member interest and almost ensure you get a full house at your next meeting.

Keys to a good system

For the treasurer, this same small act of placing an order with the brokerage firm means having to prepare a detailed financial report for each monthly meeting. But even before this can be done, the treasurer must adopt an accounting system that will permit all the club's financial affairs to be captured as accurately and as effortlessly as possible.

Indeed, a good system should be easy to implement and accomplish a few key things:

• It should allow members to quickly assess how much money they've put into the club and how effectively that money has been put to work;

• It should show in an instant how much the club has invested in different securities and what those investments are worth today;

• It should be flexible enough to accommodate new members or see an existing one depart without significant disruption to the other members;

• It should allow the treasurer to easily establish how much taxable income should be allocated to individual members; and,

• Last but not least, the financial reports flowing from the system should be easy for members to understand.

Use the unit value system

An accounting system that has the ability to do all this and more is the unit value accounting system. This is the same system used by mutual fund companies, countless investment clubs, and even by Revenue Canada. Under this system, members buy units or shares in the club with their monthly

Hot Tip

Consider putting club dues in a money market mutual fund until you are ready to invest them. That way you'll earn interest in the interim, which will make starting your accounting system more urgent.

dues, the same way you might buy shares in a company. The value of the units fluctuates from month to month, in tandem with the fortunes and ills of the club's investments. The beauty of the system is in its flexibility. You can add new members, let members contribute differing amounts, or pay out departing members with ease.

Of course, like all accounting systems, the unit value model might appear complex at first. But once you get the hang of it, you'll find it's really quite simple. In fact, understanding the unit value system greatly improves your ability to apply the financial and tax reporting techniques described in the next two sections of this book. So take the time to review the system until you understand it.

With the unit value system, you have a flexible way to keep track of the club's finances. One of the best attributes of the system is that you can implement it at any time, although it's probably best to start once your club makes its first investment. This will spare you the time — and confusion to club members — that comes from switching accounting methods midstream.

How to set up a unit value accounting system

Over the next few pages, you will learn step by step how to set up your own unit value accounting model. We'll also show you how to use the system to deal with events like adding new members or paying out departing members their fair share. Once you understand how the system works, the next section of this book will show you how to use the unit value system to design a monthly financial report that meets your club's needs.

A note about some of the calculations in the pages that follow. Most numbers reflect calculations up to three decimal points and have been rounded to the nearest 1000th.

CHAPTER 9

Set the initial unit value

If you think of your investment club as a company, then you and the other members share ownership of it in direct relation to how much money you put in. If your club has 10 members and you've all contributed the same amount over the past months, then each of you will own 10% of the club.

Another way of thinking about it, is that each of you owns shares or units in the club. Suppose that the ILC Investment Club starts out with 10 members and that each member makes an initial contribution of $50 per month. That means the total value of the club's assets in the first month is 10 times $50 or $500.

To keep the math as simple as possible, assume also that the ILC Investment Club sets the initial value of each unit at $5. (You can set any initial unit value you like.) This means the club will start out with 100 units ($500 divided by $5 per unit = 100 units), of which each member will own 10 units, or 10% of the club. The example below shows how to set the initial unit value:

Initial unit value:
Total contributions: **$500**
Divided by
Initial unit value: **$5**
Total units: **100**
Divided by
Total members: **10**
Equals
Each member's units: **10**

Buying new units

Once the club's funds are invested, they will fluctuate in value over time. This will affect the value of each club unit. If the ILC Investment Club's initial $500 grows 5% to $525 by the second month, each existing unit will increase from $5 to now be worth $5.25. Here's how you calculate the new unit value:

Unit value month two:
Securities & cash in brokerage account: **$525**
Divided by
Total units issued to date: **100**
Equals new unit value: **$5.25**

The new unit value is also the price that members will pay for new units in the club. In the second month, each member's $50 contribution will buy 9.524 units ($50 divided by $5.25 per unit). Add these 9.524 new units to the 10 each member already owns and each member now owns 19.524 units.

Most clubs recalculate their unit value based the club's portfolio value on the last business day of each month. If your club meets in the middle or late in each month, you can use the cash and securities values reflected on your most recent brokerage account statement. If you're meeting earlier than this, you might not get your account statement in time for your meeting.

If this is the case, you can use the stock quotes from a newspaper or some other source. A more recent development has been the introduction of brokerage services over the Internet. Many of these services let you access up-to-date account information by computer. This is particularly useful if members want the monthly unit value to reflect the most recent closing value of the club's portfolio. If you use invest-ment values other than those reflected on your brokerage statement, then try to have a consistent theme for the date you use. This could be the last day of the preceding month or the first business day before your monthly meeting.

Calculating your membership value

We've already seen how you buy new club units and how the value of those units is calculated. But how do you know what your total number of units is worth? The answer is to simply multiply your total number of units by the club's current unit value.

Let's assume that each of the ILC Investment Club's 10 members owns 19.524 units for a club total of 195.24 units. And let's say that by the club's third meeting, the portfolio has grown in value to $1,200. How much of this amount does each member own?

The first step is to calculate the club's new unit value. You do this by dividing the portfolio's current value ($1,200) by the total number of club units issued to date (195.24). In this case, each club unit is now worth $6.146. The example below shows each step of the calculation:

Unit value month three:
Securities & cash in brokerage account: **$1,200**
Divided by
Total units issued to date: **195.24**
Equals new unit value: **$6.146**

To know how much of the club each member owns, you multiply the units they each own (19.524) by the new unit value ($6.146). The answer is that each member owns $120 of the club's portfolio. This amount is known as the individual's membership value in the club. The example below shows each step of the calculation.

Membership value month three:
Number of units member owns: **19.524**
Multiplied by
Current value of each club unit: **$6.146**
Equals membership value: **$119.995**
or **$120**

Although the above calculation is for the club's third month, it does not include members' third month contributions. This is because you will be calculating the membership value before the third meeting and you cannot be sure that every member will attend and pay their dues. In fact, in most investment club accounting, any reports the treasurer produces always reflect transactions in the previous month. The only current figure used is when calculating the value of the club's portfolio to determine the new month's unit value.

As you will see in the next section of this book, these two things — unit value and membership value — are key components of the treasurer's monthly financial report to club members. They are calculated every month and will vary according to how the club's investments perform.

Determining a member's gain or loss

While the membership value calculation tells you how much a member's units are worth, it doesn't tell you how well or poorly the member's investment in the club has performed. To do this you must compare the member's membership value against the amount the member has actually contributed to the club.

Take the ILC Investment Club in month three again. Not counting the dues members will pay at the third month's meeting (these will be reflected in month four's calculation), each member has contributed $100. We know already that each member is going into the third month's meeting owning 19.524 units, each of which is worth $6.146. This means each member's membership value (units owned X unit value) is worth $120. The difference between what each member has contributed and the market value of their units is $20 — a gain of 20% on their investment. The example below shows the calculation.

Member's Gain/(Loss) month three:
Membership value month three **$120**
Less
$ amount contributed to date: **$100**
Equals dollar gain/(loss): **$20**
Percentage gain on $ contributed: **20% (20 ÷ 100 x 100%)**

Calculating a member's percentage ownership

Besides knowing how much their shares in the club are worth in dollar terms, members will also want to know what percentage of the club they own. With the unit value system, calculating percentage ownership is simply a matter of dividing the number of units each member owns by the total number of units the club has issued. Using the ILC Investment Club example again, each member would own 10% of the club at its third meeting. The calculation below shows how this is calculated:

Individual % ownership month three:
Number of units member owns: **19.524**
Divided by
Total number of club units issued: **195.24**
Multiplied by 100
Equals percentage ownership: **10%**

When a member misses a payment

As much as your club stresses the need for members to pay their dues on time, someone is almost certainly going to miss at least one payment. If you know you're going to miss a meeting, then it's a good idea to get your dues to the treasurer even if you won't be at the meeting. The reason for this is simply that missing a payment will affect your percentage ownership in the club. Even if you make a double contribution at the very next meeting, changes to the club's unit value might still mean your percentage ownership of the club will differ from that of other members.

Missing a month's dues affects your ownership standing.

The two membership value statements on pages 84 and 85 show what happens if Elaine misses her contribution at the ILC Investment Club's third meeting, but makes a double contribution at the fourth. Note that the first statement is what would be presented to the membership at the fourth meeting and the second at the fifth. We've assumed that the portfolio will grow by 5% before each valuation date.

The first statement shows that by missing her contribution at the club's third meeting, Elaine's percentage ownership of the club has slipped to 7.272% compared to the other members' 10.303% interest. In the second statement, you will notice that even though Elaine doubled her contribution at the fourth meeting to $100, her percentage ownership was still slightly less than the other members. This was because the unit value used to calculate how many new units Elaine can buy is higher at the fourth meeting than it was at the third.

The statements used to illustrate this example are similar in design and structure to those the treasurer will be using for monthly financial reports to the club, as explained in the next section of this book. Looking at the Membership Value Statement for month four on page 84, a few things should be readily apparent.

First, the "base units" column refers to the number of units that were outstanding after the club's second month's contributions. The column labeled "Last month's new units" refers to the units members bought with their third month's dues. The "Total units" column is the sum of the figures in the "Base units" and "Last month's new units" columns. To calculate the club's new unit value each month, you must divide the portfolio's current value by the total figure at the bottom of the "Total units" column. You will notice that the calculation is provided for members at the top of the Membership Value Statement.

When a member misses a payment

ILC Investment Club

Membership Value Statement
Month four

Portfolio value: $1,732.5 ($1,200 value in month three + $450 month three dues + 5% gain)

This month's unit value: $6.454 ($1,732.5 portfolio value ÷ 268.455 total units issued)

Name	Total dues	Base units	Last month's new units	Total units issued	Unit value this month	Member value	% Club ownership
Paul	$150	19.524	8.135	27.659	$6.454	$178.50	10.303
Ann	$150	19.524	8.135	27.659	$6.454	$178.50	10.303
Elaine	$100	19.524	0	19.524	$6.454	$126.00	7.272
Phil	$150	19.524	8.135	27.659	$6.454	$178.50	10.303
Susan	$150	19.524	8.135	27.659	$6.454	$178.50	10.303
Mike	$150	19.524	8.135	27.659	$6.454	$178.50	10.303
Joan	$150	19.524	8.135	27.659	$6.454	$178.50	10.303
Carol	$150	19.524	8.135	27.659	$6.454	$178.50	10.303
David	$150	19.524	8.135	27.659	$6.454	$178.50	10.303
Nancy	$150	19.524	8.135	27.659	$6.454	$178.50	10.303
Total	**$1,450**			**268.455**		**$1,732.50**	**100.00**

When a member misses a payment (continued)

ILC Investment Club

Membership Value Statement
Month five

Portfolio value: $2396.63 ($1,732.50 value in month four + $550 month four dues + 5% gain)

This month's unit value: $6.776 ($2396.63 portfolio value ÷ 353.672 total units issued)

Name	Total dues	Base units	Last month's new units	Total units issued	Unit value this month	Member value	% Club ownership
Paul	$200	27.659	7.747	35.406	$6.776	$239.925	10.010
Ann	$200	27.659	7.747	35.406	$6.776	$239.925	10.010
Elaine	$200	19.524	15.494	35.018	$6.776	$237.300	9.901
Phil	$200	27.659	7.747	35.406	$6.776	$239.925	10.010
Susan	$200	27.659	7.747	35.406	$6.776	$239.925	10.010
Mike	$200	27.659	7.747	35.406	$6.776	$239.925	10.010
Joan	$200	27.659	7.747	35.406	$6.776	$239.925	10.010
Carol	$200	27.659	7.747	35.406	$6.776	$239.925	10.010
David	$200	27.659	7.747	35.406	$6.776	$239.925	10.010
Nancy	$200	27.659	7.747	35.406	$6.776	$239.925	10.010
Total	$2,000	269.455		353.672		$2,396.63	100.00

Your club needs specific rules for when members resign.

When a member leaves

There are many reasons why members leave investment clubs. Sometimes they move away. Sometimes they lose interest. Dying isn't unheard of and, occasionally, a member might be kicked out for not paying their dues. Whatever the reason, one thing you need to spell out in detail from the outset is exactly what happens to the member's assets when they leave the club.

The resigning member should give written notice to one of the club's officers. The officer should then read the letter at the next regularly scheduled meeting. Club members accept the resignation and agree to pay the resigning member his or her share of the club's assets. However, the valuation of those assets should be based on the unit value at the next regular meeting after the resignation is announced. This is done to discourage people from timing their resignation to coincide with a high current value of the club's portfolio.

Another good idea is to give the club 90 days after the valuation date to pay out the resigning member. This gives the club time to build up sufficient cash from member dues to pay the departing member, rather than having to sell some of the club's holdings. While these rules apply to someone who resigns from the club, a similar procedure should be used when members want to cash in some of their units in the club.

While each investment club is free to choose its own rules within the law, there are times where circumstances may warrant the rules being relaxed a little. An example of this might be where it's clear that the departing member needs to be paid out sooner than the 90 days allowed for. Here are a number of other common practices you can use in these circumstances:

Sell the departing member's account to the remaining members.

If the departing member's account is worth 200 units for example, and there are 14 members remaining in the club, each of them would have to purchase 14.29 units to assume their share of the departing member's stake. This is a nice, tidy solution if the remaining members can afford the extra investment. It also allows everyone to retain an equal share of the club's assets.

Sell an equivalent stake to a new member.

Sometimes, the club will decide to indirectly offer the departing member's share to a new member. In this example, the new member would ante up enough cash to buy 200 units and assume an equivalent stake in the club. Those proceeds would then be used to pay off the departing member. As in the first option, this would allow the club to avoid selling investments and incurring related commission costs.

Liquidate some assets.

If there aren't any new members on the horizon and if the existing members aren't interested in taking ownership of the departing member's stake, it may be necessary to liquidate some of the club's assets. Because this might involve selling stock at a less than opportune time, and because commission expenses will be incurred to do it, clubs will often impose a modest financial penalty on the departing member to help cover costs. If you're going to sell a stock, try to be clinical about which one it will be. A good approach might be to determine through price/earnings ratios, which stock is currently the most highly priced relative to its future prospects. If the stock looks like is it fully valued and has limited potential to go higher, then chances are you might be able to repurchase the stock later on when its price is more attractive.

Whichever method your club chooses, the unit value system gives you an accurate method of determining how much the departing member is entitled to receive. The Membership Value Statement on page 89 shows you how much Paul will be paid if his resignation is accepted at the club's fifth meeting. In the table, it's assumed that Paul doesn't pay dues at the fifth meeting because he is resigning. The statement reflects the club's financial position at the sixth meeting, which is the valuation month for Paul's payout. Again it's assumed the portfolio will increase by 5% during the month.

You can see from the Membership Value Statement for month six that the club's unit value has increased to $7.115. With 35.406 units, Paul is entitled to receive a $251.91 payout. Once this money has been paid to Paul, the treasurer must remove him and all entries next to his name from the Membership Value Statement. In the interim, his holdings should continue to be factored into all calculations.

When a member leaves

ILC Investment Club

Membership Value Statement
Month six

Portfolio value: $2988.96 ($2396.63 value in month five + $450 month five dues + 5% gain)

This month's unit value: $7.115 ($2988.96 portfolio value ÷ $420.083 total units issued)

Name	Total dues	Base units	Last month's new units	Total units issued	Unit value this month	% Member value	Club ownership
Paul	$200	35.406	0	35.406	$7.115	$251.91	8.43
Ann	$250	35.406	7.379	42.785	$7.115	$304.42	10.18
Elaine	$250	35.018	7.379	42.397	$7.115	$301.65	10.09
Phil	$250	35.406	7.379	42.785	$7.115	$304.42	10.18
Susan	$250	35.406	7.379	42.785	$7.115	$304.42	10.18
Mike	$250	35.406	7.379	42.785	$7.115	$304.42	10.18
Joan	$250	35.406	7.379	42.785	$7.115	$304.42	10.18
Carol	$250	35.406	7.379	42.785	$7.115	$304.42	10.18
David	$250	35.406	7.379	42.785	$7.115	$304.42	10.18
Nancy	$250	35.406	7.379	42.785	$7.115	$304.42	10.18
Total	**$2,450**	**353.672**		**420.083**		**$2,988.96**	**100.00**

Adding a new member

The unit value accounting system's flexibility really comes into play when someone wants to join the club later on. With other accounting methods, adding a new member can be a complicated procedure. In most cases, the new member is required to contribute a large sum to be on an equal footing with the other members. If your members have been contributing $50 monthly dues for the past two years, the new member would have to fork out more than $1,200 to join.

But with the unit value system, new members can join with little more than their first month's dues and administration fee. As the Membership Value Statement for month seven on page 92 shows, Cathy joined the club at its sixth meeting, when most existing members had already each contributed $250 and owned 42.785 club units, except for Paul and Elaine whose contributions and unit holdings are different. Cathy's first $50 contribution to the club nets her 7.027 club units, which a month later are worth $52.50. Her ownership interest in the club is 1.43%.

Having uneven stakes in the club can be an issue, especially for a new member who may already feel a little inadequate about knowing less about investing than the other members. It's important for the club to make new members feel comfortable.

If a new member wants to be on an equal footing with existing members, they might be given the option of buying an equal stake in the club. This is achieved not by the new member equaling the original members' dollar contributions to date, but rather by buying an equal number of units in the club.

Adding a new member

ILC Investment Club

Membership Value Statement
Month seven

Portfolio value: $3663.41 ($2988.96 value in month six + $500 month six dues + 5% gain)

This month's unit value: $7.47 ($3663.41 portfolio value ÷ $490.353 total units issued)

Name	Total dues	Base units	Last month's new units	Total units issued	Unit value % this month	Member value	Club ownership
Paul	$200	35.406	0	35.406	$7.47	$264.52	7.22
Ann	$300	42.785	7.027	49.812	$7.47	$372.15	10.15
Elaine	$300	42.397	7.027	49.424	$7.47	$369.25	10.08
Phil	$300	42.785	7.027	49.812	$7.47	$372.15	10.15
Susan	$300	42.785	7.027	49.812	$7.47	$372.15	10.15
Mike	$300	42.785	7.027	49.812	$7.47	$372.15	10.15
Joan	$300	42.785	7.027	49.812	$7.47	$372.15	10.15
Carol	$300	42.785	7.027	49.812	$7.47	$372.15	10.15
David	$300	42.785	7.027	49.812	$7.47	$372.15	10.15
Nancy	$300	42.785	7.027	49.812	$7.47	$372.15	10.15
Cathy	$50	0	7.027	7.027	$7.47	$52.50	1.43
Total	**$2,950**	**420.083**		**490.353**		**$3,663.41**	**100.00**

Contributing different amounts

The unit value system allows members to contribute uneven amounts to the club with little extra complication for the treasurer. If a member contributes more than the other members, then he or she will simply end up buying more units each month.

This will, of course, mean that the member who contributes more will own a larger stake in the club. Be careful to avoid any one member owning more than half the club's units, since this could affect how Revenue Canada will treat the club for tax purposes (see Section 7 on page 116).

In the next section on preparing your club's monthly financial report, we have included an example where one member contributes more than the others.

Keeping Track Of The Finances

How to develop a monthly financial
report that meets your club's needs.

(Use this space to make notes for your future reference.)

The Financial Report — your club's most important document.

CHAPTER 10

Arguably the most pressing issue for club members each month is finding out how well or badly the club's investments have performed. After all, the real reward of an investment club is knowing that your time and effort is yielding fruit. That might mean a market-beating rate of return when the market's rising, or a less severe slump if it's dropping.

It's the club treasurer's duty to have this and other information ready for members at each meeting. The information is presented by way of a standard financial report, usually presented just after the previous meeting's minutes have been approved and after members hand over their current month's dues.

Consider establishing a finance committee to help the treasurer compile each month's report. This will make the club less reliant on any one person and also reduce the treasurer's workload. As an alternative, appoint an assistant treasurer.

After the constitution, the monthly financial report ranks as the club's most important working document. It details all the key information members need to know about how well their investment in the club is doing. Copies of it are distributed to each member, with a master copy kept on file for future reference. At each meeting, the treasurer should summarize key financial highlights for the month before asking the club to approve the figures. Once the report is accepted, it becomes part of the club's official record.

Besides keeping members abreast of the club's performance, the monthly financial report is critical, too, for keeping track of each member's tax liability for the year. As you will see in Section 7 on tax reporting, Revenue Canada can ask to inspect your club's financial statements at any time — even up to six years after your club has dissolved.

Retain all documents

With this in mind, it's prudent to get into a few good habits right from the start. Be sure to retain and safeguard all club documentation, including minutes from meetings and the club's constitution. Brokerage and bank statements, trade confirmations, tax slips, receipts and all official correspondence should be filed religiously. If ever Revenue Canada questions a club member's tax liability, these documents could be critical.

The treasurer must accept ultimate responsibility for ensuring that the club's financial records are in order. When the club reports to Revenue Canada, it's the treasurer's name that will be on all correspondence, so it will be he or she who is contacted if Revenue Canada has questions. This is all the more reason that a club treasurer should be chosen with care and full knowledge of the responsibilities involved.

Considering the importance of the club's financial correspondence, many treasurers like to have items mailed to them directly, either at home or to a post office box opened in the club's name. Renting a post office box is an additional cost for the club, but it is convenient if your club will be electing a new treasurer every year or two.

Tools of the trade

To create the monthly financial report, the treasurer will need to set up and maintain several statements that record the club's financial activities, including contributions by members and changes in the value of the club's investments. Set-up will take a few hours, but once complete monthly updating shouldn't take more than an hour if all the necessary information is readily available.

How you choose to prepare the club's monthly financial report is a matter of personal preference. Some club treasurers prefer a paper-based system that allows the club's books to be easily transferred periodically to new treasurers. Many others like to keep the club's financial statements on computer for quick and easy updating and printing.

A standard spreadsheet program such as Excel or Lotus 1·2·3 will be sufficient for most clubs' needs. You may encounter a few, more expensive, software programs specifically designed for investment club accounting. Most of these originate out of the U.S., so they aren't much help when it comes to Revenue Canada's reporting requirements.

The treasurer will also need access to a photocopier to prepare members' copies of the monthly financial report. The cost of copies should be covered out of the club's administrative fund in the chequing account.

Choosing valuation dates

Apart from these tools and perhaps a calculator, the only other thing the treasurer will need to prepare each month's financial report is a statement of the value of the club's investments. This might come from the club's most recent brokerage account statement or some other source.

If you use your club's most recent brokerage statement, which is the simplest solution, all values will be at least a week or two old. Clubs that use this approach often like to have the most recent newspaper stock listings available for members to assess the latest closing values of the club's investments. It's also a good idea if you're using this approach to schedule club meetings around the middle of the month. This gives the brokerage firm time to get the statement in the mail before the meeting date.

The second approach, while giving club members an up-to-date accounting of their club's financial position, requires more work for the treasurer. He or she will likely prepare the club's monthly financial report the day before the monthly meeting. Current values for each investment and any activity during the past month will have to be accessed and recorded. This may take only a few minutes if the club has only a few holdings, but it can become a chore if the club's holdings are large and varied.

While either approach is acceptable, it's best to choose one and stick with it.

A post office box will cost the club a small fee per year, but it will save the time of changing mailing addresses every time a new treasurer is appointed.

How to prepare your financial report

CHAPTER 11

Here we will show you how to set up and maintain the various financial records you will need to develop your club's monthly financial report. Since the financial report we will be building uses the unit value accounting method, be sure you have read and understood Section 5.

At its most detailed, your club's monthly financial report will consist of four forms. Each of these builds on information in the other until a full and accurate financial picture of the club's financial position emerges. Your report's first objective is obviously to keep track of how much money each member has contributed to the club. Second, you want to know how that money has been invested. Your third objective is to calculate what those investments are currently worth. And last but not least, you want to know how much of the club each member owns, what that ownership interest is worth and what gain or loss members have made on their investment in the club.

With these objectives in mind, here are the four parts to the standard financial report we recommend you use for your club:

• **Record of Dues** — simply shows how much each member has contributed since joining the club;

• **Investment Transaction Record** — describes the club's transactions for each individual investment the club owns;

• **Portfolio Value Statement** — provides details about the current value of the club's portfolio as per the brokerage account statement or more current values; and,

• **Membership Value Statement** — shows what each member's interest in the club is worth.

Now let's look more closely at each of the four statements. A completed sample of each form is provided to go with the discussion about its form and function. Blank copies of each form are also printed for your own use starting on page 159.

Record of Dues

This form keeps track of member contributions since they joined the club and for the current calendar year. As you can see by the sample on page 104, each member contributed $600 in the period before the current year. This is reflected in the "opening balance" column. The amounts members contribute in each month are entered in the corresponding columns. The last column shows the total amount that each member has contributed since joining the club.

In practice, our sample record of dues would be presented at the ILC Investment Club's February meeting. Notice that February's dues are not reflected on the form. They will only be acknowledged in the March report, after being deposited in the club's bank account and then transferred to the brokerage firm.

There is one peculiarity on this form you should take note of. David has started to contribute $75 per month in the current year instead of the $50 other members are contributing. We've included David's higher contribution to illustrate that it doesn't present any difficulty for the club since you are using the unit value accounting system. In the fourth part of the financial report, we will see how David's higher contribution will give him a bigger ownership stake in the club than the other members (see page 113).

Another peculiarity that sometimes arises is when a member misses a month's dues, but makes a single or double contribution in a subsequent month. In this case, you should enter zero for the missed month's contribution and enter the double contribution in the month it is made. Don't try to allocate money back to previous months because this will mean having to restate figures throughout the report.

Remember to always bring the club's cheque book to meetings so that you can have an authorized member co-sign cheques you will need in the coming month.

ILC Investment Club

February 15 meeting
Record of Dues

Name	Opening balance	Jan.	Feb.	Mar.	Apr.	May	June	July	Aug.	Sept.	Oct.	Nov.	Dec.	$ Total
Ann	$600	$50.00												$650.00
Elaine	$600	$50.00												$650.00
Phil	$600	$50.00												$650.00
Susan	$600	$50.00												$650.00
Mike	$600	$50.00												$650.00
Joan	$600	$50.00												$650.00
Pam	$600	$50.00												$650.00
David	$600	$75.00												$675.00
Nancy	$600	$50.00												$650.00
Cathy	$600	$50.00												$650.00
Total	**$6,000**	**$525**												**$6,525**

Investment Transaction Record

The chief purpose of this form (see page 107) is to keep a record of any gains, losses, dividends or other income the club earns from its investments. These amounts are then split between the members to declare on their income tax returns at the end of the year — even if they weren't actually received in cash.

The investment income amounts are also crucial for calculating how much capital gains tax members will have to pay if they sell part or all of their club units. Key figures in the Investment Transaction Record will be transferred monthly to members' adjusted cost base accounts, which are explained in Section 7 on page 129.

The Investment Transaction Record is split into two parts: purchases and sales. The purchases section lists all the investments the club owns. The first column shows the name of the security. You should enter information for all the club's holdings, not only those bought in the current calendar year. The second column shows how many shares or units the club owns on the date that the report is compiled.

The third column shows the purchase price, and next to it the fourth column records how much commission the club paid for the investments. These two figures are combined and divided by the number of shares to arrive at the club's adjusted cost base (ACB) per share. The ACB, essentially the total cost per share, is needed to determine capital gains or losses when the club sells an investment. See Section 7 on pages 120 to 123 for more information about calculating capital gains.

The sixth and seventh columns record dividends and interest earned from the club's investments for the year to date. Don't carry over any dividends or interest from one year to another because you could end up paying tax twice on these amounts. The last column in the purchases section shows you how much you've invested in the particular stock or fund.

In the sales section of the Investment Transaction Record, you enter details about any investments you have sold so far in the calendar year. The main reason for the sales section is to calculate capital gains or losses, which is when you sell an investment at a profit or loss. Your capital gains or losses are needed for tax reporting.

You can see from the sample record that the ILC Investment Club sold 100 shares of WIN Ltd. on January 19 for $11.25 per share (a total of $1,125). Commission on the trade was $45, which means the club actually received $1080.

To calculate what capital gain or loss the club realized from its investment in WIN Ltd., you must subtract the club's adjusted cost base for acquiring the shares. In this case, it cost the club $445 including commission to buy 100 WIN Ltd. shares, which it then sold for $1,080 including commission. That means the club has made a $635 gain on its WIN Ltd. investment ($1080 - $445 = $635).

The gain, plus the above dividend and interest amounts are carried over to each member's individual adjusted cost base account (see Section 7). This account tracks how much members have paid for their share of the club. When a member leaves the club or sells some units, the adjusted cost base will be deducted from the amount received to arrive at the member's capital gains liability.

ILC Investment Club

Investment Transaction Record

February 15 meeting

PURCHASES

Security	Shares	Price	Comm.	ACB/share	Dividends YTD	Interest YTD	$ Invested to date
A Bond Fund	100	$10.00	–	$10.00	–	$40.00	$1,000.00
FIX Co.	50	$25.50	$45.00	$26.40	$5.00	–	$1,320.00
INK Co.	100	$17.35	$60.00	$17.95	–	–	$1,795.00
MIG Inc.	25	$50.00	$45.00	$51.80	$12.75	–	$1,295.00

SALES YTD

Security	Date	Shares	Price	(Comm.)	Received	ACB	Gain (Loss)
WIN Ltd.	19/01	100	$11.25	$45.00	$1,080.00	$445.00	$635.00

Portfolio Value Statement

Club members will be keenly interested in this statement. It shows the value of the club's holdings on a specific valuation date. As mentioned earlier, you can either use the closing values on your most recent brokerage account statement, or you can use a date closer to your meeting date. In the sample Portfolio Value Statement on page 110, we have used January 31 as the valuation date. This would likely be the valuation date on the most recent brokerage account statement available for the club's February 15 meeting.

The Portfolio Value Statement serves two important purposes. It allows members to guage the club's investment performance at a glance, and it gives you the portfolio value from which to later calculate the value of each unit in the club.

The first three columns show the names of each club holding, the number of shares held and the adjusted cost base of those shares. The adjusted cost base per share is carried over from the Investment Transaction Record. A point worth special mention under the first column is the line labeled "Cash." This is the amount of cash actually in the brokerage account on the valuation date. It does not include the dues that members are going to contribute at this month's meeting. Nor does it include any cash amounts held in the club's bank account. Since you will be banking and then immediately transferring member dues to you brokerage account, any amounts in the bank are for operational expenses rather than investing.

The fourth column, labeled "Stop Loss" shows the price at which the club has set a stop loss order for the holding with the brokerage firm. This is the price at which the membership has agreed to sell the holding to limit losses or lock in gains.

You will notice that the stop loss orders are set between 10% and 15% below the holding's current value, recorded in column five. One noticeable exception on the sample statement is the stop loss for INK Co. The current market price for this stock is $36.20, while the stop loss is set almost 45% under market at $20. Obviously, this is a case where the club will need to consider locking in gains by raising the stop loss. You should make a point at every meeting to review the club's stop loss orders, but only after an update from the member responsible for tracking a stock.

The sixth column in this statement "Total cost" shows how much the club paid for its total holding of each security (number of "Shares" multiplied by the "ACB per share"). In the next column, you record the total market value of the same securities on the valuation date (number of "Shares" multiplied by the "Market price" per share). The difference between what you paid and the market value is recorded in the "$ Gain/(Loss)" column. Losses are put in brackets.

The last column in the statement simply shows the current percentage gain or loss to date on each investment and for the club as a whole. The sample statement shows that the club's portfolio has gained 33% over its original cost. This is a healthy gain, but as you will see when we look at the Membership Value Statement, the last statement in our financial report, this does not mean members' contributions have grown by the same amount.

Hot Tip

If your club has enough money, keep cash in a money market account with the brokerage to earn interest while you wait to invest it.

ILO Investment Club

Portfolio Value Statement

February 15 meeting

Valuation date: January 31

Security	Shares	ACB per Share	Stop Loss	Market Price	Total Cost	Total market value this month	$ Gain (Loss)	$ % Gain (Loss)
A Bond Fund	100	$10.00	$9.00	$9.45	$1,000	$945.00	($55.00)	(5.82%)
FIX Co.	50	$26.40	$23.00	$25.00	$1,320	$1,250.00	($70.00)	(5.3%)
INK Co.	100	$17.95	$20.00	$36.20	$1,795	$3,620.00	$1,825.00	101.62%
MIG Inc.	25	$51.80	$49.00	$53.90	$1,295	$1,347.50	$52.50	4.05%
Cash						$80.35		
Total					$5,410	$7,242.85	$1,832.85	33.88%

Membership Value Statement

Finally, the true bottom line measure of your club's performance! The Membership Value Statement on page 113 is what club members will most want to see each month. At a glance, it shows precisely how successful their investment in the club has been.

The first step in preparing the Membership Value Statement is to calculate how many units the previous month's dues bought each member. This gives you the total number of units the club has issued to date. Once you know that, you will be able to calculate the current month's unit value.

You calculate the current unit value by dividing the total value of the club's portfolio by the total number of units the club has issued. In this case, we've already seen that the ILC Investment Club's portfolio is worth $7,242.85. The total number of units outstanding is 410.367, a figure recorded in the "Total units issued" column. That means the club's February unit value is $17.65 ($7,242.85 ÷ 410.367). This is the new unit value that is used to calculate how much each member's ownership interest in the club is worth. It's also the amount that members will pay for new units in the club. Any new units members buy at the February meeting won't be shown until next month's report, where the transaction will be recorded in the "Last month's new units" column.

Now let's take a column-by-column look at what the Membership Value Statement shows:

Total dues: This is the total amount members have contributed since joining the club. The figures are taken from the last column of the Record of Dues, the first statement in the report. "Total dues" includes last month's dues but excludes dues members will pay at the current meeting.

Base units: The number of units the club had outstanding going into the previous month's meeting.

Last month's new units: How many units each member bought with their dues last month.

Total units issued: This is the sum of the "Base units" and the "Last month's new units "columns. For the next month's report, figures in this column will become the new month's base units.

Unit value this month: The calculation for this month's unit value is provided at the top of the statement. Unit value is reached by dividing the portfolio's value by the total units issued "Base units" plus "Last month's new units."

Member value: By multiplying the "Total units issued" to each member by this month's unit value, you arrive at the dollar value of each member's interest in the club.

$ Gain (Loss): The dollar difference between each member's "Total dues" and their "Member value."

% Gain (Loss): The percentage difference between each member's "Total dues" and their "Member value." This shows you how well your investment in the club has performed.

% Club Ownership: How much of the club each member owns. You calculate this by dividing each member's "Total units" by the total units issued by the club, and then multiply by 100.

ILO Investment Club

Membership Value Statement

Date: February 15

This month's unit value Portfolio value ($7,242.85) ÷ Total units issued (410.367) = $17.65

New units per contribution

$50 contribution = 2.823 units $75 contribution = 4.234 units

Name	Total Dues	Base units	Last month's new units	Total units issued	Unit value this month	Member value	$ Gain (Loss)	% Gain (Loss)	% Club ownership
Ann	$650	38.000	2.892	40.892	$17.65	$721.73	$71.73	11.04%	9.965%
Elaine	$650	38.000	2.892	40.892	$17.65	$721.73	$71.73	11.04%	9.965%
Phil	$650	38.000	2.892	40.892	$17.65	$721.73	$71.73	11.04%	9.965%
Susan	$650	38.000	2.892	40.892	$17.65	$721.73	$71.73	11.04%	9.965%
Mike	$650	38.000	2.892	40.892	$17.65	$721.73	$71.73	11.04%	9.965%
Joan	$650	38.000	2.892	40.892	$17.65	$721.73	$71.73	11.04%	9.965%
Pam	$650	38.000	2.892	40.892	$17.65	$721.73	$71.73	11.04%	9.965%
David	$675	38.000	4.339	42.339	$17.65	$747.27	$72.27	11.71%	10.317%
Nancy	$650	38.000	2.892	40.892	$17.65	$721.73	$71.73	11.04%	9.965%
Cathy	$650	38.000	2.892	40.892	$17.65	$721.73	$71.73	11.04%	9.965%
Total	**$6,525**			410.367		$7,242.85	$717.50		100%

113

Reporting on bank balances

While the club's bank balance is not the primary focus of the club's activities, it's important to keep members up to date on where the club's administrative fund stands. This doesn't require preparing a special statement, since a copy of the statement received from the bank will suffice. This can be photocopied and attached to the back of the monthly financial report.

To assist members in understanding how various amounts were spent, the treasurer should write a brief description of the expense next to each withdrawal from the account.

Using a summary financial report

In the beginning, it will likely be necessary to use the full financial report as we've detailed in the preceding pages. But as members become more comfortable with how the financial report works, you will probably find it simpler to use a summarized report.

You might also develop your own report design. This is fine since there is really no single right way to compile a financial report. So long as your report covers the key elements that we've highlighted, you can use whatever works best for you and your club.

If you will be using the method and forms we've described, then you will likely find that members will, over time, become quite familiar with how the report works. They will begin to skip over the Record of Dues and perhaps even the Investment Transaction Record. Most attention will be given to the Portfolio Value Statement and the Membership Value Statement, the two bottom-line measures of how your club is doing.

If this begins to happen, then it makes sense to start preparing a summarized financial report. Depending on how many investments your club owns, you might be able to fit all the information you need on to a single sheet. If you are using the various statements we've described in the preceding pages, then your summary report might consist of the following items:

• a brief summary of any purchases or sales in the portfolio in the past month (simply the number of shares bought or sold and the relevant dollar amounts involved);

• the Portfolio Value Statement as shown on page 110;

• the Membership Value Statement as shown on page 113; and,

• the current cash balance in the club's chequing account.

Of course, it will still be necessary to maintain a Record of Dues and an Investment Transaction Record. However, members don't have to be given these each month. Members only need to receive them at the end of the year when they will have to approve the club's financial statements, for the treasurer to prepare the club's income tax forms.

Reporting For Revenue Canada

Investment club taxation doesn't have to be hard. We show you how to do it yourself.

(Use this space to make notes for your future reference.)

Investment club taxes 101

Like most other kinds of income, you have to pay tax on the money you make from your investment club. The concept is simple enough, but in practice many investment clubs find Revenue Canada's tax-reporting requirements hard to work with. It's one aspect of running a club that almost no one looks forward to. With all those wordy documents to read, calculations to compute, and forms to fill in, you might want to dish everything over to a qualified tax accountant to take care of.

Hot Tip

Since taxes can be complicated, consider having a professional review your return for errors before you file it. This should cost only a fraction of the full cost to have a professional prepare your taxes.

However, hiring a professional is a more expensive and less fulfilling solution. Part of the investment club experience is learning to do things for yourself, so paying an accountant to do your club's taxes runs counter to the spirit and purpose of being part of a club. Of course, if your club grows large or branches into more exotic investments, then hiring an accountant can be a prudent thing to do.

For the average club, though, this section of the book contains most of what you'll need to know to keep the taxman happy. You will learn about a special provision for investment clubs called the modified partnership, and see how to go about completing the two tax forms Revenue Canada wants each year. But before we get into the detail, you'll need a bit of background to help you understand the process outlined in the rest of this section.

The first thing you should know is that there are three main types of income you can earn on investments — band each is taxed differently. These taxes are not peculiar to investment clubs. In fact, they apply to your personal investing as well.

Capital gains tax

Probably the simplest income type is a capital gain. This is when you buy an investment and it goes up in value before you sell it at a profit. The rule is that you have to pay tax on 75% of the profit. If you make a $100 profit selling a stock, then you will have to pay tax on $75. How much of that $75 will go to taxes depends on your personal tax bracket. If you're in a 40% tax bracket, then you'll pay $30 in taxes (40% of $75), which leaves you with $70 on your $100 capital gain.

Of course, calculating your capital gain is not as simple as subtracting the price you paid for the shares from the price you sell them for. There are added costs to take into account, such as brokerage commissions. The price you pay for the shares plus the brokerage commission when you buy gives you the shares' adjusted cost base. If you buy 100 shares of DEF Co. at $35 for a total of $3,500 and pay $50 commission, then the adjusted cost base for the shares is $35.50 ($3,500 + $50 ÷ 100 shares).

If two years later you sell your 100 shares of DEF Co. at $50, you would take your adjusted cost base plus the commission from the sale into account before determining your capital gain. Assuming that you pay $60 commission to sell the shares, then you would compute your capital gain using the following simple formula:

Gross proceeds on sale (100 x $50)	**$5,000**
Less: Cost of shares including commission	**$3,550**
	= **$1,450**
Less: Commission on sale	**$60**
Capital gain	= **$1,390**
Taxable capital gain (75% of $1,390)	**$1,042.50**

Sometimes your club will own shares in a company that were bought at different times for different prices. This might happen if the club votes to buy more of a particular stock because of a favorable change in its business operations. So how do you calculate capital gains when this happens?

The answer is known as the *average cost method.* You calculate this by adding the cost base of all the shares and dividing that number by the total number of shares you own. Taking DEF Co. again, say your club decides to buy 200 more shares when they have risen to $38 from $35. This is how you would calculate the new adjusted cost base for the 300 DEF shares the club now owns:

Initial 100 DEF Co. shares at $35 plus $50 commission =	**$3,550**
Second 200 DEF Co. share at $38 plus $70 commission =	**$7,670**
Total cost	= **$11,220**
	Divided by: 300 shares
	Equals: $37.40 per share

The opposite of a capital gain is a capital loss. This is when you sell something for less than you paid. You can use 75% of any incurred capital losses against your taxable capital gains. So if you have $100 in taxable capital gains and the same amount of legitimate capital losses, you can apply the losses to the gains and not have to pay tax. You can also carry capital losses to future years, or apply them against gains you made up to three years earlier.

Two twists on the capital loss rules are important. First, you can only claim a capital loss on an investment if you actually get rid it of by selling or transferring it in writing to someone else. If you buy shares in a company that goes bankrupt and the shares become worthless, you either have to sell the shares for whatever you can get or give them away before you can record the capital loss.

You also can't claim a capital loss against capital gains if you sell an investment at a loss and buy it again within 30 days. Also, if you bought the shares within 30 days of selling them and still own some 30 days later, you cannot claim the capital loss. If you later sell all the shares, then you might be able to claim the full capital loss.

Capital gains taxes are a central theme of most investment club tax reporting. They crop up in more places than you might expect, and we go into more detail about them later.

Dividends tax

The second most common income type for investment clubs is dividends from qualified Canadian companies. This is the most favored type of investment income. Depending on your income tax bracket, you may end up paying less tax on dividends than other income types.

This is because of the federal dividend tax credit, a tax break that effectively encourages Canadian residents to invest in the country's businesses. Only dividends of listed Canadian companies qualify for the dividend tax credit.

A company pays dividends to shareholders out of after-tax profits. Since the money has already been taxed in the company's hands, Revenue Canada treats dividend income favorably. A four-step formula is used to determine dividend taxes. First the dividend amount is "grossed up" — increased — by 25%. That means federal tax on dividends of $100 would be based on $125 ($100 plus 25%). The extra $25 is called the gross up. From the federal tax you would owe, you can deduct the federal dividend tax credit. The credit is a variable percentage of the grossed-up dividend of $125. The final step in the formula is calculating how much provincial tax you must pay. That amount depends on where you live and what tax bracket you're in. Generally, dividend income enjoys slightly better treatment than capital gains, but this might not be so in Quebec, where a different formula is used.

The dividend gross up and the federal tax credit are shown on the T5 form a company sends each year to shareholders, or in this case, to the investment club. Most often your brokerage firm will issue the T5 form on the dividend issuer's behalf. It may also combine all the club's dividends for the year on one T5 form, which simplifies matters for the club treasurer.

Tax on interest

Since most clubs invest in stocks, you're unlikely to accumulate significant amounts of interest income. If you do, though, then you pay tax on the full amount of interest at whatever your personal tax rate is. If you're in the 40% tax bracket and earn $100 in interest, then you will pay $40 in tax (40% of $100), leaving you with $60.

If your club borrows money to invest — something we strongly advise against — then the interest on the loan may be deductible against the interest received on the investment.

Each year, the club treasurer must allocate to club members the capital gains, interest and dividends the club has received. The fairest allocation is to split each amount according to the percentage each member owns of the club's assets. Members will get a form from the treasurer showing their share of the three kinds of investment income. This you will file this with your personal income tax return.

Choosing the modified partnership structure

Modified partnership makes taxes easier

Legally, each member of an investment club owns what's called an *undivided interest* in each of the club's investments. If the club owns one share of QRS Ltd. and there are 10 members in the club, then each member owns 1/10th of that share. If the club sells the QRS share and realizes a taxable capital gain of $1, then each member must report 1/10th of the gain or $0.10 on his or her tax return.

CHAPTER 13

This is fine except that things get complicated if the club trades stocks regularly, admits new members, sees members leave or lets members contribute uneven amounts. This can become an impossible situation, needing complex mathematical calculations.

In fact, so difficult can the "undivided interest" issue be that even the skilled accountants at Revenue Canada realized something had to be done to ease the burden on bona fide investment clubs. After all, investment clubs exist for pursuits more pleasurable than plugging away at complicated math problems. That is why Revenue Canada has since 1973 allowed bona fide investment clubs to choose to be taxed as a partnership, which is a type of business structure.

This means each member owns a partnership interest in the club rather than an undivided interest in each club investment. Capital gains, dividends and interest collect at the club level as if it were a separate entity. They are then distributed to each club member in a reasonable manner to report on their tax returns. This streamlines the number of calculations needed to determine capital gains or losses.

Since a club is not legally a partnership unless it's registered as one, Revenue Canada terms a club that chooses to be taxed as a partnership a "modified partnership." The main benefit of choosing to be treated as a modified partner-ship is that you enjoy the simpler partnership tax treatment without formally having to register one. Using the unit value accounting system explained in Section 5, it's easier under this structure to add new members, let members contribute uneven amounts and trade securities frequently.

How a club becomes a modified partnership

Revenue Canada says only bona fide investment clubs can choose to become a modified partnership. The rules for what constitutes a genuine club are clear. In practice, most ordinary investment clubs would qualify. A club is considered bona fide when:

• All members are individuals;

• Most members are not from the same family;

• Family members did not, at any time, own more than 50% of the outstanding club units;

• Most of the club's assets consist of cash, shares, bonds or mutual funds; and,

• Sales of club property will give rise to capital gains or losses.

If your club meets these criteria, then there are three other rules all members of the club will have to agree to follow:

1. To use the modified partnership basis of reporting and to compute the income of the club on a calendar year basis;

2. To accept the club treasurer's statement of income and the amount taxable in the hands of each member including capital gains and losses; and,

3. That records will be kept of the adjusted cost base of each member's "partnership interest" in the club.

The last point is important. Essentially it means there are two ways investment club members can be liable for capital gains tax. The first is when the club sells an investment at a profit. The second is when the member sells or cashes in part or all of his or her club units.

Calculating the adjusted cost base for a member's partnership interest in the club is different than computing it for an investment. Revenue Canada sets out a specific formula that modified partnerships must use to keep track of each member's adjusted cost base.

If your club meets the criteria of a bona fide club and all members agree to the above three conditions, then becoming a modified partnership is straightforward. All that remains is for the treasurer to indicate in a letter to the local tax office that your club wants to be treated as a modified partnership. A sample letter is included on page 163.

All club members should sign the letter, which you should file with the club's annual Partnership Information Return, form T5013. There is more information about when and how to complete the Partnership Information Return and supplementary documents later in this section. When new members join the club, a similar letter should be filed to indicate they, too, accept the modified partnership basis.

Calculating members' adjusted cost base

If you choose to be treated as a modified partnership, then you must keep records of the adjusted cost base of each member's interest in the club. This lets you determine members' capital gains or losses when they dispose of their club units.

The formula Revenue Canada dictates may seem complicated at first, but once you put it in practice you'll find it quite straightforward. After all, there's an incentive for club members to use the formula. If you did not use it, then members would end up paying tax twice on dividends, interest and capital gains they received during their years of club membership.

Here' s how you calculate each member's adjusted cost base:

ADD:

1. The member's total contributions to the club, except for loans the member might have made to the club.

2. The cost the member paid for units bought from other club members.

3. The member's share of the excess of capital gains over capital losses in a year (100% of the gain or loss).

4. The member's share of interest and dividends in a year without grossing-up dividends from taxable Canadian corporations.

5. Capital dividends allocated to the member in a year (these are rare for clubs since private corporations pay them).

From the above total amount, you then:

SUBTRACT:

1. Any withdrawals the member makes from the club such as a withdrawal of part of capital or all or part of income, except where the member sells or otherwise disposes of club units.

2. The member' s share of the excess of capital losses over capital gains in a year (100% of the gain or loss).

3. The member's share of any net loss in income in a year (e.g. where interest charges on a loan exceed interest earned on the investment.)

4. If the member disposes of some but not all of his or her units, the member's adjusted cost base of those units.

The reason you must keep track of each member's adjusted cost base is to determine how much capital gains tax they must pay when they sell their club units or the club cashes them in. A member who sells club units must declare three quarters of the difference between the proceeds from the sale and the adjusted cost base of those units.

If the club has to sell investments to pay out a departing member, then part of any gain or loss on the sale of the holdings may or may not be allocated to the member who is leaving. If no gain or loss is allocated to the leaving member, then the total gain or loss will be split among the remaining members. This means that the people remaining will receive a higher proportion of the gain or loss because it is spread between fewer individuals.

So what happens when a new member joins the club? The member's starting adjusted cost base is the price paid for the units. The price of the units would include any unrealized capital gains in the club's assets at that time. If the club later realizes all or part of these gains, the new member will be subject to tax on the amount attributed to him or her. This can come as a surprise to members who have been with the club for only a few months and who have not seen a significant growth in their unit value. If this happens in your club, point out that the taxes will be recovered when the member sells his or her units in the club. This is because the unrealized capital gains have been included in his or her adjusted cost base, which will reduce the amount of capital gains realized when the member sells.

How to file your club's tax returns

CHAPTER 14

Getting started

Investment clubs that choose to be treated under the modified partnership rules must file the same information with Revenue Canada that business partnerships do. This means you will have to complete two types of forms — one for the club and one for each member.

One exception is if your club has fewer than six members. In this case you don't have to file these forms, although nothing precludes you from doing so. At a minimum, Revenue Canada requires members of modified partnerships that have less than six members to attach their club's financial statements to their tax return. These should indicate how much income you earned from the club during the year.

For clubs of six members or more, Revenue Canada requires that you file the two types of forms. The first is the T5013 Summary, which gives an overview of the club's results for the year. For modified partnerships the year-end is December 31. The T5013 Summary also shows how much income from the club has been allocated to the members on the second form, the T5013 Supplementary.

The four-part T5013 Supplementary gives each club member information about the investment club's results for the year. It includes details about income, losses, and other amounts allocated to the member. Club members use the T5013 Supplementary to prepare their annual personal income tax return. The club treasurer must complete a separate T5013 Supplementary slip for each club member. Samples of these two forms are included on page 164.

Since these two forms are intended for formal business partnerships, many of the requested entries are irrelevant to an investment club. However, you will still find the free information guides that accompany these forms useful and fairly easy to follow. You can get these from any Revenue Canada office. Forms and the guide are also available on the Revenue Canada Web site at **www.rc.gc.ca**.

While on the Web site you can also get a copy of the modified partnership guidelines for investment clubs, known as the special release to Information Circular 73-13. Unfortunately, the tax people haven't gotten round to putting this document into language most of us can understand. Fortunately, the explanation we've provided in this book has done that for you. But if you want to read the original, it' s there on the site. Just type "investment clubs" into the site's search engine and links to the relevant information will pop up on the screen.

The other thing you will need to get started are club members' social insurance numbers. Revenue Canada can fine your club $100 each time a SIN is not shown on an information slip. Members of investment clubs have to give their SIN to the person preparing the tax forms, which is usually the treasurer. Members who don't are liable for a $100 penalty each time they refuse. If a member does not have a SIN, they must apply for one. Only members under 18 years of age and whose total income is less than $2,500 are exempt from this rule.

The club treasurer, or whoever else is completing the tax returns, has a responsibility to safeguard the use of members' SIN numbers. Any person who misuses an individual's SIN number or gives it to someone else without consent is liable to a stiff fine, imprisonment, or both. We mention this not to scare you, but to illustrate the seriousness of the treasurer's role and responsibilities.

Completing the tax forms

The job of completing the T5013 Summary and T5013 Supplementary will be made much easier if your club's records are accurate and up to date. If you have followed the unit value accounting system explained in Section 5 and the financial reporting method detailed in Section 6 of this book, then you should have no trouble at all.

Since this will be your club's first return, remember to include the letter which all members have signed agreeing to have the club treated as a modified partnership. The sample letter is included on page 163.

The logical place to start is with the T5013 Summary, which describes your club's operational results. From the information on this form you will extract the relevant figures for the T5013 Supplementary forms for each member.

The T5013 Summary must be filed with Revenue Canada by March 31. You must also have distributed the T5013 Supplementary slips to club members by the same date. Given these deadlines, it's a good idea to make sure your club meets in January so that you can approve the club's financial statements. This will allow the treasurer to begin completing the tax forms to have them ready for the February meeting. This will satisfy those members who prefer to file their personal income tax returns early rather than waiting until the April deadline.

The process of completing the two tax forms is fairly straightforward for most investment clubs. Most get along fine by simply following Revenue Canada's guide. Of course, since these forms weren't specifically designed for investment clubs, there are a number of things that might spark confusion. If you're confused about something, you're best advised to put in a call to your local tax office.

Distributing the forms

Once you've completed the T5013 Summary and the T5013 Supplementary forms, you will need to distribute them.

To Revenue Canada you must send:

• The original copy of the T5013 Summary form;

• The top copy of all the T5013 Supplementary slips;

• One copy of the club's financial statements for the year; and,

• Any other forms or documents that might be relevant.

   To each club member you must give:

• Copies 2 and 3 of the T5013 Supplementary slip. The text on the back of the slip tells the member how to use the information.

For the club's records, you must keep:

• A copy of the T5013 Summary;

• Copy 4 of the T5013 Supplementary slips for all club members; and,

• Copies of any attachments you are sending to Revenue Canada.

   Details of which Revenue Canada office to send your return to are contained in the relevant Revenue Canada guide. Once your return has been received, Revenue Canada will automatically assign a filer identification number to your club. You should use this number in all future correspondence with your tax office.

Books and records Revenue Canada says you must keep

Your club must keep sufficient records of its activities so that Revenue Canada can verify the amounts allocated to individual members. For investment clubs, these books and records should include:

• Bank and brokerage account statements, trading confirmations, T5 forms, invoices, receipts and other documents to support proof of your club's transactions;

• The club treasurer's regular monthly financial reports, including the adjusted cost base of each member's interest in the club; and,

• Your club's constitution or a partnership agreement.

The club has to keep books and records for at least six years after the end of the last fiscal period to which they relate.

When your club shuts down

At some point, club members may decide to shut down the club. If this happens, you will have to file your club's final tax return. The club's investments will be liquidated and the money fairly distributed to the remaining members.

Completing the final tax return for the club and the members is a little more complicated than usual. Any income such as interest, dividends and capital gains from the club's investments must be allocated to the members to declare on their personal income tax returns. In addition, any capital gain members earn by redeeming their interest in the club must also be declared.

If the club discontinues its operations on or before the end of the year, you have to file any outstanding return, by the earlier of 90 days after the date the club folds or March 31, even if your club has already filed one tax return in the year. If your club shuts down on March 31, 2002, you will still have to file your return for the year to December 31, 2001. You will then have 90 days to file a return for the period from January 1, 2002 to March 31, 2002.

Even after your club dissolves, you are expected to hold on to the club's records for six years.

Investment Club Resources

Sources to help you become sharper
at spotting winning investments.

Notes (Use this space to make notes for your future reference.)

Learning is key to success

Nothing can replace the thrill of researching and investing in a hot stock. But the reality is that, while memorable, such occasions will be few and far between — even for the most talented of stock pickers.

However, you can improve your chances — and maintain member interest in the club — if your club fosters an environment of ongoing education. And believe us, there's almost no limit to the new things you can learn about investing.

Here are some ideas and sources that can help your club become more savvy investors:

CHAPTER 15

Enlist your broker's help

Investment advisors can be your best allies in learning how to invest. With years of expertise and experience, they can help your club identify promising sectors and companies to research. They can also provide your club with information on industries or companies from their firm's research department. Generally, these reports are available free to the firm's clients. Many brokers are accustomed to offering educational seminars for clients on subjects like how to analyse stocks or properly manage a portfolio. If your broker is eager enough about your club's business, he or she will gladly attend a club meeting to deliver a presentation on a specific topic. Brokers network with other professionals like accountants and lawyers, so they can also arrange for these people to talk to your membership.

Most of all, though, a good broker can act as a mentor to your members, advising and teaching them about the capital markets and answering questions.

If you use a discount brokerage, you won't have a specific broker. However, most discount brokerages go out of their way to give clients access to a large variety of research and other educational products — often for free or at very attractive discounts. Many also run free educational seminars in their branches.

Many discount brokerages publish catelogues of investment research and educational tools that you can get at big discounts to their regular prices.

Investment research services

A number of companies sell independent investment research to investors. Generally, you subscribe to a service and receive updated data in the form of printed sheets, or electronically on-line or on diskette. Companies generally offer both stock data and mutual fund information.

Subscriptions to some of these services can be costly, although some large public libraries have subscriptions, in which case you get the service for free. More recently, companies have packaged cheaper versions of their vast databases to attract individual investors. Most of these services are accessible only over the Internet. If you are thinking about subscribing to an Internet-based service, make sure it's from a firm that has a track record in the business.

If you want to subscribe to a stock research service you can consider one the services of the **Financial Post Datagroup**. They have a wide array of different products, the flagship of which is their *Investor Reports* service, which provides current and historical information on 500 Canadian public companies. For more information, you can call the Financial Post Datagroup at (416) 350-6507 or 1-800-661-POST (7678).

Another prominent service, the *Blue Book of CBS Stock Reports*, provides research and analysis on 255 Canadian companies, with 32 updated reports every two weeks. Published by **MPL Communications**, a leading Canadian publisher of investment research, the Blue Book is one of the more affordable products for investment clubs. For more information, call (416) 869-1177.

There are also a number of firms active in Canada that provide research data on U.S.-listed stocks. The best-known two are **Standard & Poor's** (S&P) and **Value Line**. S&P

Hot Tip

Some discount brokerages provide clients with free use of independent research services that track both Canadian and U.S. stocks. You can also get industry and economic data from them for free.

offers its *Stock Reports* service on the Internet, tracking 4,600 U.S.-listed companies. Value Line issues its 1,700-company service in print and on CD-ROM, with updates available on the Internet.

If you're looking for in-depth mutual fund data, then you have a wider number of sources to choose from. Portfolio Analytics (1-800-531-4742) distributes the popular *PalTrak* mutual fund research software. The other popular software-base mutual fund research tool is *BellCharts* (416-515-4757). Both of these products are updated monthly and allow you to compare mutual funds on a variety of fronts, including past returns, expenses and their portfolio structure. Several other organizations and publishers also offer mutual fund analysis products, most of which are updated less frequently than PalTrak or BellCharts.

Since any of these products will more than satisfy the most active club's needs, you needn't spend much time assessing which ones to buy. That time would be better spent trying to find the cheapest price.

Not to be overlooked is the old-fashioned way of conducting your investment research by getting annual reports from the companies you're interested in. Because most companies will gladly send you their reports free (and probably other material as well), this is still the cheapest investment service we know of.

Order annual reports from companies at their Web sites. Or better still, download the annual report on-line and save yourself time and effort.

Investment newsletters

Literally hundreds of investment newsletters today offer subscribers advice on what stocks to buy or avoid. Many focus on a single investment style, stock type or size, or on stocks in a particular industry. Unless your club plans to specialize in one area, you'd probably do better to look for a more general investment newsletter.

Two such products are available from MPL Communications, the same people who produce the *Blue Book of Stock Reports* mentioned earlier. *Investor's Digest of Canada* is a twice-monthly newspaper ideal for generating investment ideas for your club. It is filled with topical articles, educational features, interviews and research summaries from many of Canada's leading brokerage analysts.

The second advisory, *Investment Reporter*, offers specific advice on which stocks to buy and which to avoid. It is published every two weeks.

Using the Internet

Nowhere is the glut of information about investing more apparent than on the Internet's World Wide Web. The trouble is trying to separate the wheat from the chaff — the practical and useful sites from the promotional marketing-driven ones.

Of course, the Internet being the ever-changing medium it

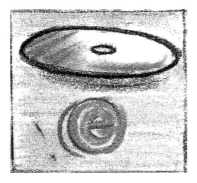

is, it's always difficult to offer a list of recommended sites without overlooking a number of excellent ones. Here, nonetheless, are a few free sites definitely worth your club's time.

For researching Canadian public companies start with *Carlson On-line* (**www.fin-info.com**) before linking to *SEDAR* (**www.sedar.com**) Carlson, operated out of Vancouver, is a pioneer in bringing several useful sources of

Compile an annual list of topics members want to know more about, then use part of the club's annual administrative money to pay for books, seminars and field trips on these subjects.

company information together on a single site. Here you can search for public companies by market capitalization or industry type. Once you've found companies of interest, you can view their latest news releases, get stock quotes and charts, visit a discussion forum on the company and link to the company's own Web site. Carlson also allows you to link to the stock exchange where the company is listed, as well as to SEDAR, a database of official corporate disclosure documents.

SEDAR is where you go when you want in-depth information on a particular company. All public companies legally have to file information with the provincial securities commissions about activities and events that can have a material affect on their business. When they do, this information is stored in the SEDAR database.

For free mutual fund information, two sites deserve special mention. They are ***Globefund.com (www.globefund.com)***, a service of The Globe and Mail newspaper which features articles and mutual fund data, and the ***Fund library (www.-fundlibrary.com)*** which hosts very similar information.

Investment seminars and courses

Since educating members is a key mandate of most investment clubs, you should familiarize yourself with the various sources of investment education in your community.

Many ***community colleges and universities*** offer night

school investing classes at reasonable rates. The not-for-profit *Investor Learning Centre of Canada* (1-888-452-5566) regularly offers a two-level seminar program called *Intelligent Investing* in a growing list of communities across the country. Led by expert instructors, these educational courses include a host of valuable reference materials and books

Two other sources for periodic educational seminars, publications and free brochures are the major *stock exchanges* and the provincial government *securities administrators.* The latter also host periodic community activities such as public town hall meetings and information sessions. See page 167 for contact information.

Your local *public library* may also be a resource for investment books and periodicals. In Toronto and Calgary, the Investor Learning Centre runs free *Resource Centres* for investors which include free Internet access, stock research databases and data subscription services, as well as hundreds of reference books, free brochures and periodicals. The Toronto Resource Centre is located downtown at 121 King Street West, and the Calgary Resource Centre is located in the Calgary Public Library.

For the investor who wants to gain a professional-level understanding of investing, the *Canadian Securities Institute (CSI)* offers a number of self-study courses that are open to the public. These include the Canadian Securities Course™, a prerequisite for professional licensing to sell securities and a gateway to the CSI's more advanced programs.

Most brokerages subscribe to expensive corporate data services. Ask your broker to supply you print outs on the companies you're interested in.

The Canadian Securities Course is a registered trademark of the Canadian Securities Institute.

Books and periodicals

Being part of an investment club often pushes you into the habit of reading the financial press, particularly if you're responsible for keeping tabs on one or more of the club's investments.

While your local daily newspaper is fine for the main business news of the day, for more extensive coverage you need to turn to the specialist financial press. In Canada, the two major financial daily news sources are *The Financial*

Post section of the *National Post* and the *Globe and Mail's Report on Business,* both of which also publish monthly magazines. Two Canadian magazines — *Canadian Business* and *Profit* — have dedicated followings.

Several U.S. magazines are also worth investigating. *Fortune* (twice-monthly), *Money* (monthly), *Worth* (monthly), *Forbes* (monthly), *Individual Investor* (monthly) and *Smart Money* (monthly) are available on most newsstands.

Also in the periodical category you can include a number of *market reviews* published monthly by Canada's stock exchanges. These give you a variety of key trading and other data on listed companies and indices.

Stripping down the many investment books to only a handful of titles is more difficult. There are scores of excellent titles, each of which has its own merits. At the very least, club members will need to learn the basics of investing and of analysing stocks by reading financial statements.

The list that follows includes several publications by the Canadian Securities Institute, the publisher of this book. No bias is intended by including them; they're simply relevant titles you will want to consider.

• *A Random Walk Down Wall Street;* Malkiel, Burton G.; W.W. Norton & Co., 1990.

• *Bulls and Bears;* Anderson, Hugh; International Thomson Publishing, 1998.

• *Common Stocks and Uncommon Profits and Other Writings;* Fisher, Philip A.; John Wiley & Sons, 1996.

• *Getting Started in Stocks;* Hall, Alvin D.; John Wiley & Sons, 3rd Edition, 1997.

• *How to Invest in Canadian Securities*; Canadian Securities Institute; 7th Edition, 1997.

• *How to Read Financial Statements;* Canadian Securities Institute; 5th Edition, 1998.

• *Investments Crash Course*: *What Every Canadian Should Know About Investing;* Canadian Securities Institute, 1998.

• *Security Analysis* (Classic 1934 Edition); Graham, Benjamin; Dodd, David L.; McGraw-Hill, 1997.

• *The Bottom Line Guide to Investing;* Canadian Securities Institute;1998.

• *The Intelligent Investor;* Graham, Benjamin; Harpercollins, 4th Revised Edition, 1997.

• *The New York Institute of Finance Guide to Investing;* New York Institute of Finance, 1992.

Appendix A

Please complete this questionnaire frankly and fully. Your answers will help our club develop a sound investment policy and ensure that the club meets the expectations of all members.

How would you describe your investment experience and knowledge?

a) Know nothing   b) know a little   c) know a lot   d) expert

Which of the following investments have you personally bought in the past?

a) GICs   b) CSBs   c) Mutual funds   d) Stocks   e) Options or futures

How would you describe your investment personality?

a) Very conservative   b) conservative   c) aggressive
d) very aggressive

If the club makes some bad investments, how much of your money would you be prepared to lose?

a) all of it   b) three-quarters   c) half   d) one quarter
e) none of it

If you had the choice, which of the following would you choose?

100% chances to win $100
50% chance to win $1,000
10% chance to win $10,000
1% chance to win $100,000

Which of the following investments should our club consider buying (choose no more than two).

a) Mutual funds   b) Stocks   c) Bonds   d) Options
e) Futures

How much should each member contribute to the club at each meeting?

a) $15   b) $25   c) $50   d) $75   e) $100

Should members be allowed to contribute different amounts?

a) Yes   b) No   c) Don't know

Please indicate which of the following club positions you are interested in holding?

a) President   b) Vice-President   c) Treasurer   d) Secretary
e) none

Have you belonged to an investment club before?

a) Yes   b) No

How often should the club meet?

a) every two weeks   b) monthly   c) every two months
d) quarterly

What times would best suit you for club meetings (please write day and times)

Day of the week_____Time of day_____

Please provide the following additional information:

Name:_____

Day Tel: (_____)_____   Night Tel: (_____)_____

Address:_____

_____

_____

_____

Appendix B
Sample constitution
for the ILC Investment Club

Before you finally agree on a constitution, it is a good idea to consult a lawyer to make sure your constitution is clearly worded.

1. Formation of Club. The individuals signing this constitution are forming an investment club. The name of the club is

_____.

2. Purpose of Club. The club's purpose is to teach its members how to evaluate securities and to invest members' periodic contributions of money for their mutual benefit.

3. Duration. The club will begin on_____(date) and will continue to operate until it is dissolved as provided by this constitution.

4. Meetings. Meetings of the club will be held at a frequency to be determined by the club. Members will decide on the times and places for the meetings.

5. Club dues. Each member must make a monthly contribution to the club. The monthly contribution amount will be decided by a two-thirds majority vote of the members. If a member is delinquent in his or her monthly contributions for a period of more than 61 days, the member may be terminated from the club by a two-thirds majority vote of the members. The terminated member will receive an amount subject to the terms described in Section 13 of this constitution, less the contributions not paid up to the date of termination.

6. Administration fee. Each member must make an annual contribution to the club to defray the club's administrative costs. The annual contribution amount will be decided by a two-thirds majority vote of the members.

7. Club structure. By signing this constitution, club members agree to have the club treated as a "modified partnership" for tax purposes under the conditions prescribed by Revenue Canada.

8. Management. All club members are expected to participate equally in the management of the club and attend no less than two out of every three club meetings. Club decisions will be made by a two-thirds majority vote of the members required to form a quorum, except as otherwise required by this constitution. A quorum will consist of two-thirds of the members of the club. A member who is absent from a meeting may vote by signed proxy assigned to a member attending a meeting.

9. Officers. Club members will elect by a simple majority vote the following officers of the club:

• A president who will chair all meetings.

• A vice-president who will do the president's duties in the absence or incapacity of the president.

• A secretary who will keep the club's records and prepare written minutes of meetings and decisions of the membership.

• A treasurer who will establish and maintain a bank account and an investment dealer account in the club's name and make monthly reports on the club's financial position to the members. The club may name one or more officers in addition to the treasurer to have authority to withdraw funds and execute orders from the club's bank and brokerage firm account. The treasurer will keep written accounts of the club's transactions, which any member can examine. The treasurer will prepare and distribute to members, according to the time limits prescribed by Revenue Canada, all appropriate documentation required for reporting income tax liabilities, including keeping and maintaining an adjusted cost base account for each member.

Officers will carry out other duties normally associated with their positions or as directed by resolution of the membership.

Officers will serve for terms of one year unless otherwise prescribed by resolution of the membership and until their successors are elected. Any officer may be removed by a two-thirds vote of the entire membership during his or her term of office.

10. Investment dealer. Club members shall vote to select an investment dealer or securities broker to execute orders placed by the club's authorized officers. By resolution, the members will designate the club's officer or officers authorized to buy or sell securities through the dealer or broker. The dealer or broker may rely on the resolution until it is modified or rescinded in writing. Stocks, bonds and securities the club owns will be left with the broker or dealer to be held in "street name" for the club's account. Any corporation or transfer agent called upon to transfer any securities to or from the name of the club is entitled to rely on instructions or assignments signed by a designated officer or officers of the club without inquiry as to the authority of the person(s) signing such instructions or assignments, or as to the validity of any transfer to or from the name of the club.

11. Compensation. No officer or other member shall be compensated for services given to the club, except for reasonable and necessary club expenses authorized by a vote of the members.

12. New Members. The club may admit additional members at any time by unanimous consent of all members, so long as the total number of members is not more than 25. As a condition of membership, all members agree to be bound by the terms of this constitution and by all resolutions adopted or to be adopted by a vote of the members.

13. Withdrawal of Members. A member may withdraw from the club at any time. Death or legal incapacity of a member will be considered a voluntary withdrawal. A withdrawing member must give written notice to the club's secretary or any other officer. The effective date of withdrawal will be as of the next regularly scheduled club meeting, which will also be the date for valuing the withdrawing member's interest in the club. Between receiving the withdrawal notice and the subsequent withdrawal valuation date, other members may buy, in proportion to their membership interest in the club, the interest of the withdrawing member. Club members may, during this same period, agree by unanimous consent to sell the withdrawing member's interest in the club to a new member who has not yet established an interest in the club. If the other members decide not to buy the withdrawing member's interest in the club, or sell the interest to a new member by the valuation date, the club will use cash on hand or sell securities to pay the withdrawing member the value of his or her interest in the club, less the cost of selling securities to obtain the cash necessary to meet the withdrawal. The withdrawing member shall be paid in cash, but without interest, not later than ninety (90) days after the valuation date.

14. Nonassignability of Member's Interest. No member may assign, transfer, pledge or hypothecate his or her membership or interest in the club, in whole or in part, and any attempt to do so shall be construed as such member's election to withdraw from the club.

15. Amendment of Constitution and Dissolution. This constitution of Club may be amended or the club may be dissolved upon a two-thirds affirmative vote of the entire membership at any regular or special meeting, provided that written notice of the proposed amendment or proposed dissolution has been given to each member at least fourteen (14) days prior to the meeting. On dissolution, all the club's debts and expenses will be paid first, and the club's remaining assets will be distributed to the members in cash or in kind, or partly in cash and partly in kind, apportioned in accordance with the membership interests of the members.

IN WITNESS WHEREOF, the founding members have signed and executed this Constitution of Club the_____day of _____, _____, at ___(City and Province)_____.

1. Name

Signature

2. Name

Signature

3. Name

Signature

4. Name

Signature

5. Name

Signature

6. Name

Signature

7. Name

Signature

8. Name

Signature

9. Name

Signature

10. Name

Signature

Note: All founding members must sign this document.

Appendix C

ILC Investment Club   __/__/__

<u>Monthly Stock Review Sheet</u>

Security: _____

Stock exchange: _____   **Shares held:** _____

Recent price: _____   **52 week Hi/Lo:** _____

Adjusted Cost Base: _____

Dividend Yield: _____   **P/E:**_____

Target sell P/E:_____   **Stop loss:**_____

Recent news: _____

_____

_____

_____

_____

_____

My recommendation: _____

_____

Club's decision: ____voted to hold.

____voted to sell ____ shares @ $_____

____voted to buy____ shares @ $_____

____voted to increase/decrease

stop loss to $_____

Appendix D

Record of Dues

Meeting date: _____

Name	Opening balance	Jan.	Feb.	Mar.	Apr.	May	June	July	Aug.	Sept.	Oct.	Nov.	Dec.	$ Total
Total														

Investment Transaction Record

Meeting date: _____

PURCHASES Security	Shares	Price	Comm.	ACB/share	Dividends YTD	Interest YTD	$ Invested to date

SALES YTD Security	Date	Shares	Price	(Comm.)	Received	ACB	Gain(Loss)

ILC Portfolio Value Statement

Meeting date: _____
Valuation date: _____

Security	Shares	ACB per Share	Stop Loss	Market Price	Total Cost	Total market value this month	$ Gain (Loss)	$ % Gain (Loss)
Cash								
Total								

Membership Value Statement

Meeting date: _____

This month's unit value

Portfolio value (_____) ÷ Total units issued (_____) = $ _____

New units per contribution

$ _____ contribution = _____ units $ _____ contribution = _____ units

Name	Total Dues	Base units	Last month's new units	Total units issued	Unit value this month	Member value	$ Gain (Loss)	% Gain (Loss)	% Club ownership
Total									100%

Appendix E

Revenue Canada

(Address)

(Date)

   We the undersigned are the members of the (Your club's name), a bona fide investment club as described in paragraph 7 of Information Circular 73-13 Investment Clubs.

   We hereby elect the modified partnership basis of tax reporting and agree to follow the conditions outlined in paragraph 5(a) to (c) of Information Circular 73-13 Investment Clubs.

Member Name: (signature)_____

Date:_____

Member Name: (signature)_____

Date:_____

Member Name: (signature)_____

Date:_____

Member Name: (signature)_____

Date:_____

Member Name: (signature)_____

Date:_____

Appendix F

<table>
<tr><td>Revenue Canada / Revenu Canada</td><td>**PARTNERSHIP INFORMATION RETURN**</td><td>Page 1</td></tr>
</table>

Complete this return using the instructions in the *Guide for the Partnership Information Return.*

For departmental use
1616

Area A – Identification

Information return for fiscal period From:	Year Month Day	To:	Year Month Day		

Partnership's identification number

Business Number

Tax shelter identification number

Partnership's name (please print)

Care of

Head office address

City	Province or territory	Postal code

Country

Have you filed a partnership information return before?   no 1   yes 2

If *yes*, for what year: 19 _____

Address on last information return, if different from above

City	Province or territory	Postal code

Country

Is this a limited partnership?   no 1   yes 2

If *yes*, provide the name and address of the principal general partner.
Name

Address

City	Province or territory	Postal code

Country

Location of books and records
Address

City	Province or territory	Postal code

Country

Name of partner designated under subsection 165(1.15) of the *Income Tax Act*

Departmental use

50 ☐☐☐☐

Total number of T5013 Supplementary slips attached:

51

Partnership's principal business activity:

52   Professional ☐   Business ☐   Rental business ☐

Commission ☐   Farming ☐   Fishing ☐

Other ☐   Specify: _____

Jurisdictions where partnership operates:

53   ☐ ☐ ☐
      ☐ ☐ ☐
      ☐ ☐ ☐

Is this the final information return for the partnership?

54   no 1   yes 2

Was the partnership inactive **throughout** this fiscal period?

55   no 1   yes 2

Please state the language of your choice for correspondence:

56   English 1   French 2

Did you pay someone to prepare this information return?

57   no 1   yes 2

Area B – Certification

Person to contact for more information

First name ——— Surname ———	Area code ——— Telephone number ———
58	59 ( )

I, _____ , certify that the information in this return and in any documents attached is, to the best of my knowledge, correct and complete, and fully discloses the partnership's income.
(Please print)

Date	Authorized partner's signature	Position or office

T5013 Summary E (97)   (Ce formulaire existe aussi en français.)   3651   Canadä

Area C – Summary of partnership's income or loss

Business income	Gross	170	...... Net	171	
Professional income	Gross	172	...... Net	173	
Commission income	Gross	174	...... Net	175	
Farming income	Gross	176	...... Net	177	
Fishing income	Gross	178	...... Net	179	
Total business income	Gross	180	...... Net	181	
Rental income (non-business activity)	Gross	200	...... Net	201	
Total income	Gross	310	...... Net	311	

Capital cost allowance	220	
Actual amount of dividends from corporations resident in Canada	240	
Interest from Canadian sources	250	
Foreign dividend and interest income	260	

Real estate: Capital gains or losses	270	Reserve	280	
All other: Capital gains or losses	271	Reserve	281	
Total: Capital gains or losses	272	Reserve	282	

Business investment loss	290

Area D – Selected data from partnership's financial statements

Gross profit	400		Management fee expense	401	
Subcontract costs	402		Interest expense	403	
Advertising and promotion	404		Repairs and maintenance	405	
Salary and wages paid (excluding salary or wages to partners)				406	

Area E – Miscellaneous information

Is this partnership a member of another partnership? 500 no 1 yes 2

If yes, please give the name, address, and identification number of the other partnership.

Name 501	Partnership's identification number 502
Address 503	

City 504	Province or territory 505	Postal code 506

Are any members of this partnership also a partnership? 507 no 1 yes 2
If yes, tick the boxes to indicate the type of end members: individuals ☐ trusts ☐ corporations ☐

Are any members of this partnership non-residents? 508 no 1 yes 2
If yes, did the partnership:

• file an NR4 return for tax deductions withheld at source for the fiscal period; and 509 no 1 yes 2
If yes, provide the non-resident account number. 510

• issue NR4 Supplementary slips to the non-resident partners? 511 no 1 yes 2

Did the partnership make any elections under the Income Tax Act during the fiscal period? 512 no 1 yes 2
If yes, attach a copy of the election.

If the partnership reports rental income, is the rental property the principal residence of any of the partners? 513 no 1 yes 2
If yes, provide that partner's name. 514

Did the partnership have any scientific research and experimental development expenditures? 515 no 1 yes 2
If yes, attach a completed Form T661.

Did the partnership earn any investment tax credits (ITCs) during the fiscal period? 516 no 1 yes 2
If yes, enter the total ITCs earned, and attach a completed Form T2038. 517

Did the partnership incur any exploration and development expenditures during the fiscal period? 518 no 1 yes 2
If yes, enter the total expenditures. 519

| | Revenue Canada | Revenu Canada | | STATEMENT OF PARTNERSHIP INCOME
ÉTAT DES REVENUS D'UNE SOCIÉTÉ DE PERSONNES | | | T5013
Supplementary
Supplémentaire |

Fiscal period end Exercice se terminant le Month / Mois Year / Année	09	Tax shelter identification number Numéro d'inscription de l'abri fiscal	10	Partnership's identification number Numéro d'identification de la société de personnes	11	Partnership code Code du genre de société de personnes	12	Business code Code du genre d'activité

| 13 | Partner's share (%) of partnership income (loss)
Part (%) de l'associé dans les revenus (pertes) de la société de personnes | 14 | Recipient code
Code du genre de bénéficiaire | 15 | Country code
Code du pays | 16 | Member code
Code du genre d'associé | 17 | Recipient's identification number
Numéro d'identification du bénéficiaire |

Partner's name (surname first) and full address
Nom, prénom et adresse complète de l'associé

Partnership's name and full address
Raison sociale et adresse complète de la société de personnes

18	Canadian and foreign net business income (loss) Revenu net (perte nette) d'entreprise canadien et étranger	19	Foreign net business income (loss) Revenu net (perte nette) d'entreprise étranger	20	Canadian and foreign net rental income (loss) Revenu net (perte nette) de location canadien et étranger	21	Foreign net rental income (loss) Revenu net (perte nette) de location étranger	22	Capital cost allowance Déduction pour amortissement

| 23 | Limited partnership loss available for carryforward
Perte comme commanditaire disponible à reporter | 24 | Actual amount of dividends from corporations resident in Canada
Montant réel des dividendes de sociétés résidant au Canada | 25 | Interest from Canadian sources
Intérêts de source canadienne | 26 | Foreign dividend and interest income
Revenu étranger en dividendes et en intérêts | 27 | Capital gains (losses)
Gains (pertes) en capital |

| 28 | Capital gains reserve
Réserve relative aux gains en capital | 29 | Business investment loss
Perte au titre d'un placement d'entreprise | 30 | Income tax deducted
Impôt sur le revenu retenu | 31 | Partnership's total gross income
Revenu brut total de la société de personnes | 32 | Carrying charges
Frais financiers |

| 33 | Foreign tax paid
Impôt étranger payé | 34 | Charitable donations and government gifts
Dons de bienfaisance et dons au gouvernement | 35 | Cultural and ecological gifts
Dons de biens culturels ou écosensibles | 36 | Federal political contributions
Contributions politiques fédérales | 37 | Provincial political contributions
Contributions politiques provinciales |

| 38 | Investment tax credit
Crédit d'impôt à l'investissement | 39 | Canadian exploration expenses
Frais d'exploration au Canada | 40 | Canadian development expenses
Frais d'aménagement au Canada | 41 | Canadian oil and gas property expenses
Frais à l'égard de biens canadiens relatifs au pétrole et au gaz | 42 | Foreign exploration and development expenses
Frais d'exploration et d'aménagement à l'étranger |

Details – Détails

| 43 | Recapture of earned depletion
Récupération de la déduction pour épuisement gagnée | 44 | Amount eligible for resource allowance deduction
Montant donnant droit à la déduction relative aux ressources | 45 | Limited partner's at-risk amount
Fraction à risques de la participation du commanditaire |

For tax centre
Pour le centre fiscal **1**

T5013 Supplementary - Supplémentaire (97)   2794   Canadä

Appendix G

Canadian Securities Administrators

Alberta
Calgary
Tel: (403) 297-6454   Fax: (403) 297-6156

Edmonton
Tel: (403) 427-5201   Fax: (403) 422-0777

British Columbia
Vancouver
Tel: (604) 899-6500   Fax: (604) 899-6506

Manitoba
Winnipeg
Tel: (204) 945-2548   Fax: (204) 945-0330

New Brunswick
St. John
Tel: (506) 658-3060   Fax: (506) 658-3059

Newfoundland
St. John's
Tel: (709) 729-4189   Fax: (709) 729-6187

Northwest Territories
Yellowknife
Tel: (867) 920-6964   Fax: (867) 873-0243

Appendix G

Canadian Securities Administrators (continued)

Nova Scotia

Halifax

Tel: (902) 424-7768   Fax: (902) 424-4625

Ontario

Toronto

Tel: (416) 593-8314   Fax: (416) 539-8122

Prince Edward Island

Charlottetown

Tel: (902) 368-4569   Fax: (902) 368-5283

Québec

Montréal

Tel: (514) 873-5326   Fax: (514) 873-3090

Saskatchewan

Regina

Tel: (306) 787-5645   Fax: (306) 787-5899

Yukon

Whitehorse

Tel: (867) 667-5005   Fax: (867) 393-6251

Index

C

D

More Books From The

Investor Learning Centre
OF CANADA

Order today for you or a friend!

The <u>Bottom Line</u> Guide to Investing

The perfect starting point for new investors, this easy to read 50-page book cuts through the clutter to give you the common-sense essentials of investing. You'll learn the key points on stocks, bonds and mutual funds, discover tips for hiring a financial advisor, and learn simple steps to give your retirement savings a boost.   **Price: $9.95**

Investment Terms and Definitions

Ever wanted to know the meaning of a new investment term? This handy pocket-size dictionary can help with straightforward explanations of securities jargon from A-Z   **Price: $6.95**

How to Read Financial Statements

A company's financial fitness is the most important consideration when you're thinking about investing in its stock. This compact guide explains in simple terms how financial statements work, and how by crunching a few numbers you can unlock valuable insights into a company.
Price: $14.95

How to Invest in Canadian Securities

An invaluable investor's resource for more than 27 years, How to Invest in Canadian Securities contains over 200 pages of market wisdom gathered over the years by the respected Canadian Securities Institute. It explains the facts on mutual funds, stocks and bonds and offers sound tips on how you can retire comfortably.   **Price: $25.95**

Prices exclude GST/HST and are subject to change without notice. Shipping charges may apply.

To order by credit card call 1-888-452-5566 or buy online at www.investorlearning.ca.